HOW TO BE A
SOCIAL DIVA

AN ESSENTIAL GUIDE FOR THE GIRL ABOUT TOWN

Peg Samuel
with Lexi Tabback

EASTON
STUDIO PRESS

U.S. Edition published by
Easton Studio Press
P.O. Box 3131
Westport, CT 06880
(203) 454-4454
www.eastonsp.com

ISBN-10: 0-979824-88-5
ISBN-13: 978-0979824-88-3

www.socialdiva.com

Printed in Canada

First Printing: March 2009

10 9 8 7 6 5 4 3 2 1

Book design and cover by Turtle Island, Inc. (www.turtleisland.com)

We dedicate this book to
all the Social Divas out there…
You are our inspiration—
and you look FABULOUS today!

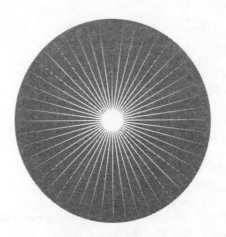

CONTENTS

INTRODUCTION

The phone rings. It's your friend from New York and she has super-duper VIP backstage passes to the MTV Awards. She informs you that she told her chisel-faced boyfriend to take a hike for one night because she wants *you* to be her date.

Do you go?

Wait…did you really just ask yourself that?

Because whether or not you're going is a complete non-issue.

You're going. No question.

And you're going because you might never have another chance to hang with Kim Kardashian, Rihanna, Lauren Conrad and the rest of the gang backstage at Radio City.

The only issue we see here is that you need to pack a bag and hop on the red-eye as quickly as your Jimmy Choos can carry you!

At this point you might be thinking to yourself, "How will I get to the airport? Who will feed the cat while I'm away? Wait, forget the cat…what shoes will I take?"

Alas, this is also the part of the story—regretting the fact that you paid your rent this month instead of buying that Prada dress. What's even worse is that you're probably about to stress out to the point where all the Botox in the world could not uncrease your forehead.

(Insert super-heroinesque music here.)

The Social Divas are here to save the day—and, more important, your forehead!

In this book we are going to help you to solve all the devastating little dramas that crop up daily in your busy life.

Have a wardrobe crisis? Here you'll find Social Diva wardrobe guidelines for any and every event, from a friend's house party to a red carpet soirée.

Have an accessory calamity? We'll give you tips of the Social Diva trade, such as how to fit your life into a clutch bag, or how to get away with not carrying a bag at all.

We're Peg Samuel and Lexi Tabback—and we're Social Divas and your new best friends! This book is your essential guide for living, breathing and, most important, shopping like a Social Diva.

But before we delve into the depths of Diva-hood (please note our killer alliteration skills), perhaps we should tell you a little bit about who we are and why we are qualified to school you in the ways of the Diva.

Peg Samuel is the president and founder of Social Diva, the informative website where this book originated, and is affectionately referred to as The Diva.

Even before the inception of Social Diva in 2000, Peg was known around Atlanta as the go-to girl for everything from where to find the best selection of Manolo Blahniks to which restaurant serves the most delicious risotto.

So, in order to cut down on her phone bills, she created www.socialdiva.com to keep all her pals—along with everyone else in Atlanta—in the know about…well, just about everything.

Taking things a step further, Peg began to produce her own events—giving the Atlanta social scene something worth talking about—and promoted them through her website. Word spread like wildfire, and aspiring Divas from all over Atlanta started to show up for Peg's events. And, just like that, the Social Diva phenomenon began to take hold of the entire town.

Lexi Tabback entered the realms of Diva-dom in 2002. One day, while flipping through one of her favorite magazines, she noticed a listing for a "Martinis and Manicures" event in Atlanta. Looking more closely, she saw that the event was being produced by a company called Social Diva—a sassy name indeed. It caught her eye not only because of its undeniable cuteness, but also because Lexi was on the lookout for an internship with an event marketing company.

Figuring that it couldn't hurt to visit the contact page on the Social Diva website and ask (or, if you want the truth, beg) for a six-month placement, Lexi e-mailed Peg the following:

> Dear Ms. Samuel,
>
> My name is Lexi Tabback and I am currently a junior at Kennesaw State University. I desperately need an internship to complete my major requirements, and your company seems like it would be a wonderful fit for me.
>
> That said, could you use some *free* help? If so, please call me.
>
> Thanks,
>
> Lexi Tabback

So, after a quick coffee meeting at which Lexi charmed Peg's socks off—and because Peg is The Diva and knows never to pass up the free stuff—Lexi had her internship and Peg had a minion to do her bidding. (Just kidding.)

One semester later, after some hard work and an obscene amount of sweet-talking on Lexi's part, Peg invited Lexi to drop her intern title and become Social Diva's resident wordsmith. From then on Lexi was recognized around town as Peg's little protégée, but was better known to the insider crowd as Baby Diva.

In the months to come, Peg and Lexi ran amok all over Atlanta. Well, not so much amok—they just threw a lot of parties… and they were really awesome parties. We're talking restaurant and boutique openings, movie premieres, spa gatherings, lingerie parties—you name it. And if they didn't throw the bash themselves, they were arriving fashionably late and looking better than anyone else in the joint.

Then, after a year or two of being Atlanta's go-to girls for making life fabulous, Peg packed her bags for New York to launch Social Diva: NYC, leaving Lexi to her own brilliant devices with Social Diva: Atlanta. Later the website would encompass both the East and West Coasts, attracting some serious attention. Then one day, a brilliantly astute Diva turned to them and said, "You know, you guys should write a book."

So we did.

And now you're reading that book.

Crazy, right? We know.

But now that you're up to speed, we can get down to what it means to be a Social Diva.

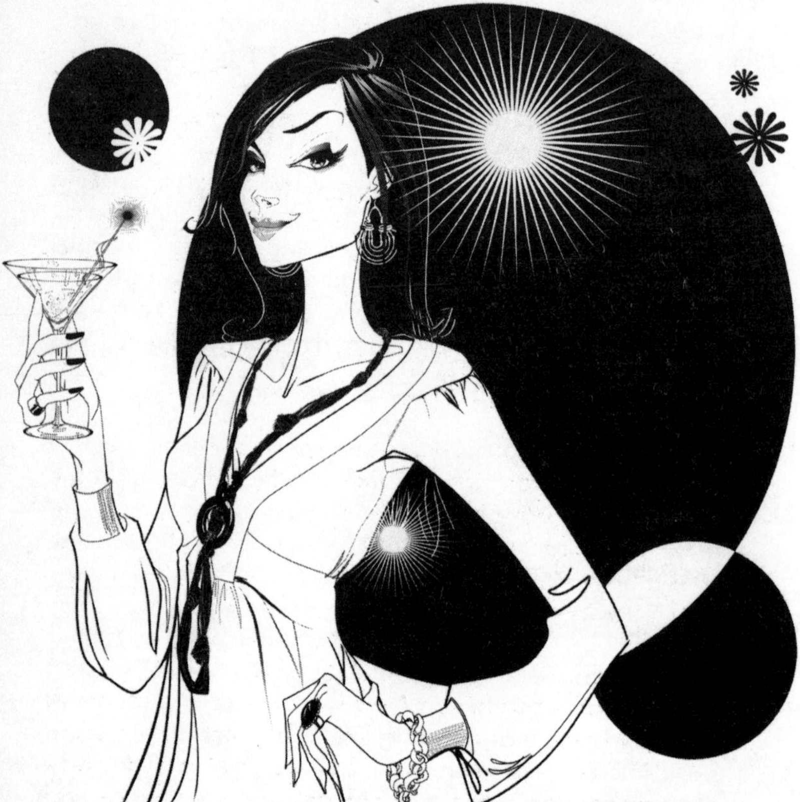

Chapter One
DIVA FUNDAMENTALS
How a Social Diva Does...EVERYTHING

Understand, being a Diva isn't just about singing arias or being an ill-tempered bitch any more. It's a certain style, a strut, an attitude—and we know all about what it is and how to get it—and we usually get it at a discount, or better yet, for free.

So before you begin on your road to Diva-dom, you need to know a few guidelines right off the bat.

First of all, we need to make one thing perfectly clear: Being a Social Diva starts from within. When you feel amazing on the inside, you shine on the outside. Having a positive attitude and self-confidence can get you far in any social situation, whether it's a cocktail party at a friend's house, a networking event in a grand ballroom, or a backstage bash at a rock concert.

Second, it is crucial to recognize that being a Social Diva also means some physical upkeep. Now, we're not talking spending twenty-four hours a day looking like a Dior model, but some basic maintenance is necessary in a Diva's daily routine. Think about how you feel when you look down at your hands and your nails are done perfectly, or when you glance in the mirror and realize your waxing specialist finally got the arch in your eyebrow just right—doesn't that give you a certain glowing satisfaction inside? Wait, why did we even ask you that? *Of course* it does…you're a Diva!

Essential Social Diva Maintenance

To make things a little easier, we've made a list of the crucial products and treatments you'll need to stay looking and feeling like a Social Diva 24/7.

Hair cut and color
Split ends and dark roots are complete no-nos. Remember, ladies, while men have their cars, women have their hair. Make sure yours always looks like a Ferrari, not a Hyundai.

Manicure and Pedicure
Yes, even in the winter. You never know when you might have to slip off your stilettos in front of a cozy fireplace—you certainly don't want to be caught with icky winter feet. Oh, and please make sure that the varnish on your nails and toes is the same color. Mismatched digits take away from that look-at-her, she's-so-together image you're going for.

Facial
Divas must have clean pores (see Diva Commandment No. 5, page 17)—this is basic hygiene, plus it keeps you looking younger (i.e., wrinkle-free) longer.

Massage
Divas don't do knots, especially knots in the muscles. A deep tissue massage will keep you supple, and drinking a good amount of water afterward will remove toxins from the body

(which got there, no doubt, from the obscene number of martinis you've consumed over the past ten years).

Teeth whitening
A nice smile is a necessity. It's amazing how far you can get—and how much you can get away with—by flashing a 200-watt Colgate smile.

Makeup
Keep your makeup appropriate for the context: light and simple to run out and get a cup of coffee; more dramatic if you're going to a movie premiere. But even if you wear nothing else, always, always, always wear lipstick or lip gloss. It brightens up your whole face and gives you the extra bit of confidence you just might need if you run into Mr. Hottie McHotness on the way to pick up your latte.

Eyebrow waxing, threading, or plucking
Your brows frame your face, and imperfect eyebrows are the equivalent of hanging the *Mona Lisa* on the bathroom wall of a Winnebago—*sooo* not OK. Eyebrow upkeep is absolutely essential. Even if you're down to your last $20, we insist you use that money to get your brows professionally done.

Body waxing, shaving, or lasering
Nobody likes a furry Diva. Unless you live in a commune and smell of patchouli (which you probably don't, since you're reading this book), you must shave and/or wax the following body areas:

- legs (lower and upper)

- bikini line

- underarms

- upper lip

- chin

- big toes (you know, those little wiry hairs that grow just below the first joint—and don't deny you've got them!)

The only time it is completely appropriate for a Diva to sport fur on her body is if it's attached to some item of clothing, such as a coat, and even then we suggest going faux.

Now that you have your inner and outer beauty in line with the Diva cosmos, we can move on to the final requirements for Diva-dom—the Ten Commandments that all Social Divas live by, or at least do their very best to follow.

The Ten Commandments of Diva-dom

1. Thou shall always accept a free cocktail.
When someone offers you a drink, you will accept it graciously, especially if he's adorable. However, if said cocktail-provider is a troll, still accept the drink, and then excuse yourself politely. Remember, he's the one who wanted to buy, you didn't ask for it; therefore you don't owe him anything except a thank you.

2. Thou shall always order the lobster.

Whether it's going on your card or someone else's, you know you deserve it, so stop mulling over the menu and order what you *really* want.

3. Thou shall always carry an iPod.

Because you never know when someone might ask you to play DJ at an impromptu gathering.

4. Thou shall fear no sample sale.

Divas scoff in the face of the bottomless bins and overflowing racks of designer merchandise, because a true Diva knows that the three-and-a-half-hour search will be well worth the finds.

5. Thou shall always maintain clear pores.

We hardly need tell you that blackheads are unacceptable, so if your Biore strips can't handle the job, get thee to the esthetician…ASAP.

6. Thou shall never waste time when there is shoe shopping to be done.

There is a time to walk the dog, a time to put away the groceries, and even a time to dust, but as a Diva, you must hand those duties over to those better suited to do them (you know, someone like the guy across the hall who has an almost embarrassing crush on you), and spend the majority of your time shoe shopping.

7. Thou shall speak no blasphemy of the Divas of Yore.

Never, ever under any circumstances, should you or anyone around you verbally assault the Divas of Yore. They are your foremamas, and you must show respect. The only exception to this Commandment is nasty talk of Diana Ross's wig (because it is simply atrocious).

8. Thou shall always push for the upgrade.
Divas do not fly Economy class, and Divas do not stay in any hotel room that does not offer 300-count Egyptian cotton sheets. There is always a way to get an upgrade. Your job is to find it, learn it, live it, and love it!

9. Thou shall always collect the free swag.
You can always use another nail file, and your boyfriend can always use another ugly T-shirt to wash your car with.

10. Thou shall love thyself.
Because thyself is fabulous!

Test Your Diva-ness

Now that you know the basic Diva guidelines, the Diva Ten Commandments, and all that we strive for, the time has come to test yourself on how much of a Diva you already are and find out how much help you need from us.

Answer these five questions, then follow the scoring directions at the end of the quiz.

1. Your rent is due in two days, but as luck would have it, on your way home from work you come across a Jimmy Choo sample sale. What do you do?

a. Keep walking. Your landlord will not take your shoe addiction as an excuse for delinquent payment…again.

b. Look in the window but don't go in. There's no harm in staring from afar; plus you just bought a pair of Jimmy's last month.

c. Go in, but promise yourself you won't buy anything. Look around for a bit, then completely disregard your original thought and buy a pair of fabulous hot-pink strappy sandals.

d. Say to yourself: "Rent? What rent? What's the point of having a place to go home to if it's not filled with gorgeous things like Jimmy Choo's!" Then spend your rent money, your food money, and max out your credit card on ten pairs.

2. Your birthday is approaching and you call the poshest restaurant in town to book a table for your pre-party nosh session. What do you say to ensure you get the best table in the joint?

a. "Hi there, I need to reserve a table for ten for next Thursday."

b. "Hello, my birthday is next Thursday, and all my friends are coming in from out-of-town to celebrate. Could I please reserve a table for ten on that date?"

c. "Hi, this is Ms. Dita Divalicious and I'm a writer for *Foodie* magazine. I'd like to bring a few friends to dine in your establishment this coming Thursday, and we need to book a table. Oh, by the way, could you alert your head chef and manager that we'll be reviewing your restaurant?"

d. "Hi, this is Ms. Dita Divalicious from Totally Fake Public Relations. I'm calling on behalf of someone who is very, very VIP. So VIP, in fact, that I can't even tell you her name over the phone—you know how those paparazzi are so sneaky nowadays! We need a table for ten for next Thursday, under the name Lips Magnificent. Please make sure you have your best champagne chilling, and that we get the best table in the house. We'd also like to request that the maître d' serve us himself, and that the head chef prepares all our food. I'm sure this won't be a problem, correct?"

3. You're all decked out and on your way to the grand opening of the soon-to-be hottest club in town. But when you get to the door you find that you're (gasp!) not on the list. What do you do?

a. Leave.

b. Ask the doorman to check the list again, and then have him check for the names of the friends you are with. When he still comes up empty, you politely thank him for looking, leave, and head to a different club.

c. Flash your old student ID and claim that it's a press pass. Then you inform the doorman that you're from *Clubbers Gone Wild* magazine and that you would hate to have to write about how unacceptable your experience was at this club.

d. You wouldn't know, you have never needed to be on the list because the club owner always escorts you through the door personally.

4. You call your favorite spa to make an appointment to get your eyebrows done. But, much to your dismay, she can't fit you in for the next three months. What do you do?

a. Find a new eyebrow girl and move on with your life.

b. Ask her to notify you of any cancellations, then take out your tweezers and pluck the strays yourself until you can get in.

c. State that this is impossible because you have a standing appointment for an eyebrow shape-up every two weeks.

d. Call your waxing specialist on her cell—you have the number because, well, you have *everyone's* number—and offer to pay her extra after hours or on her day off (which she wouldn't accept because she would *never* let you walk around with unshapely eyebrows).

5. You're making your rounds at a super-upscale event. You're dancing, you're mingling, you're networking—you know, just being you. All of a sudden, disaster strikes when the heel of your stiletto breaks off. How do you handle this one?

a. Go home and cry with embarrassment (and for your recently deceased shoe).

b. High-tail it to a secure area (i.e., your car or the ladies' room) and call a friend who lives close to the party venue. Describe what you're wearing and ask her to swing by with a pair of shoes that would match your outfit.

c. Break off the heel on your other shoe to make them match—flats are *sooo* hot right now!

d. Pull your emergency shoes out of your Gucci hobo bag and slip them on. You always carry an extra pair just in case of a situation like this. Oh, and then make a note on your Blackberry to call Michael Kors on Monday and ask him to send you a new pair…for free.

HOW TO SCORE YOUR DIVA LEVELS
Mostly 'a' answers = Devoid of Diva
You have some work to do if you want to be a Social Diva, but that's what we're here for. The biggest perk of being a Diva is that you pretty much get whatever you want, which is something that you're obviously not used to, since your answers to the quiz indicate that you're a bit of a pushover. We suggest that you do not leave the house until you've read this book cover to cover, *at least twice*. In fact, you should carry this book with you wherever you go. Think of it as a map to getting what you want.

Mostly 'b' answers = Wannabe Diva
OK, so sometimes you push for the upgrade to First Class, but you always end up in Economy anyway. You have the right idea, you're just not sure how to use it yet. Kick that confidence up a notch, find yourself some "industry" friends, and you'll be on your way to Diva-dom in no time.

Mostly 'c' answers = Diva-licious
You have it, girl! And by "it" we mean everything. You're smart, intelligent, witty, prepared, organized, and utterly fabulous! You get things done, but you don't push it too far, and that's what we

like about you. Although you're fantastic just the way you are, everyone can always use a few more tips on how to score free shoes. Stick with us, kid, we'll make you a super-duper Diva yet!

Mostly 'd' answers = Super-Duper Diva

You're like the Obi Wan Kenobi of Diva-dom! You might use this book for a tip or two, but then pass it on to one of your less Diva-fied friends. Or, if you feel like nodding your head in agreement for a while, you can read the next eleven chapters. By the way, could you tell Madonna and Angelina we say hello?

Now that we've schooled you in the basics, it's time to get a little more specific. We're about to take you through the world of a Diva and give you step-by-step instructions on how to entertain, travel, shop, eat, look, party, and relax like one of us.

Roll out your Mont Blancs, ladies, because Social Diva is a lifestyle. And we're about to show you how to live it!

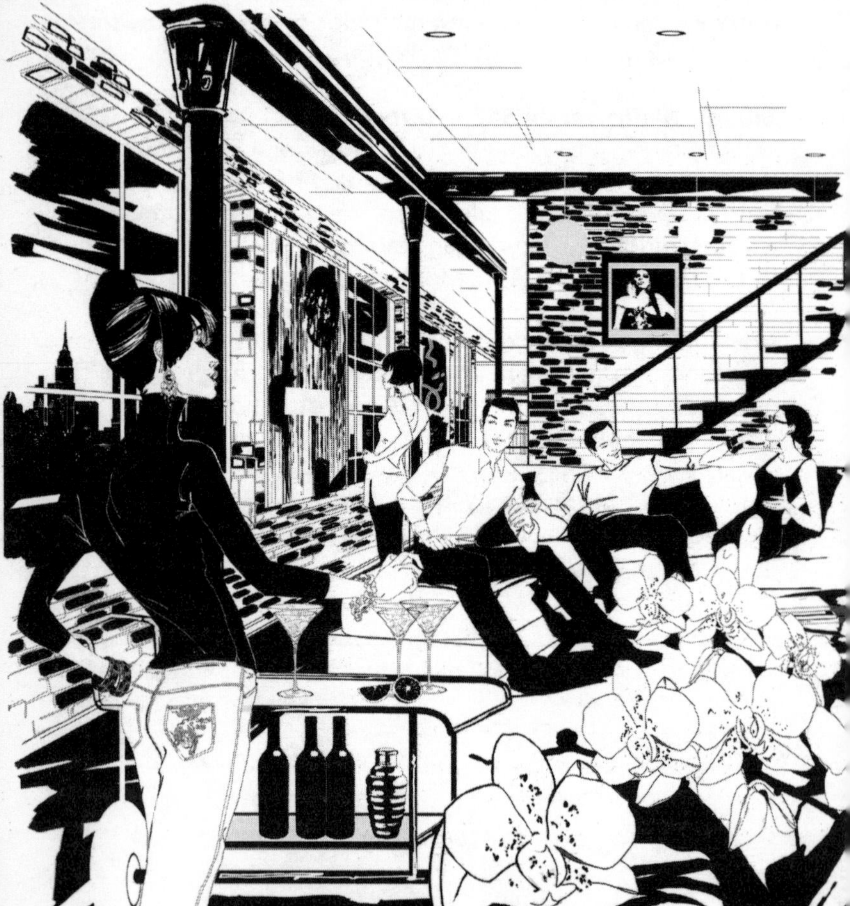

Chapter Two

IF YOU GIVE GOODIE BAGS THEY WILL COME

How a Social Diva Entertains at Home

Nothing worthy of note happening in your town? Sick of shelling out hard-earned cash paying for taxis? Doomed to another boring Saturday night at the same old place? Fret not! When there's nothing to do, Social Divas do their own thing—and their own thing (in case you didn't know) is throwing the ultimate party of the season.

Social Divas attend parties all the time, so throwing a swinging soirée of their own comes as second nature. In this chapter we'll examine all the little things a Diva has to bear in mind when planning a saucy shindig, including what kind of party to throw, who to invite, what to serve, entertainment options and, most important, how to make it all come together fabulously.

Fight for Your Right to Party (And for No Apparent Reason at All)

Social Divas never need a reason to throw a party, but it's good to have one nonetheless. With a party purpose in mind, you'll find it much easier to create a theme, decorate your pad, and make a guest list.

When deciding on your party purpose, don't delve too deep, Diva! Seemingly ordinary, everyday occurrences are reason enough to party for a Social Diva. For example, let's say you finally found your long-lost car keys—throw a "Lost and Found Fete" for you and the rest of your forgetful friends. Finally reached your target weight at the gym? Cook a fantastic dinner for your pals and call it a "Cheat (on Your Diet) Feast." Did you buy a new house? Throw a "Reception For Those With Not-As-Bad-As-We-Thought Credit Ratings." Finally worked out how to use your TiVo? Invite your circle to a "Gala for the Technologically Inept."

Now, if you happen not to feel particularly creative and simply can't think of a good reason to party, there are always plenty of life events and calendar holidays available to schedule a celebration around. But, as a Diva, you know that when it comes to hosting a gathering that revolves around a well-known event or date, you can't just throw any old party—you have to throw *the* party; with an interesting twist. Here are a few different get-togethers you can host in place of your typical holiday or life-event shindig.

Diva-Fy Your Party

THE EVENT…	ANYONE ELSE WOULD…
A friend's birthday	…throw a birthday party, complete with cake, presents and, quite possibly, a male stripper dressed as a policeman.
Valentine's Day	…sit at home and sulk about being lonely on the big V-Day.
The arrival of the Summer Season	…throw a pool party or a barbeque.

A SOCIAL DIVA WOULD...	THE DEAL...
...throw an **Un-Birthday Party**, complete with cake, presents, and most definitely a male stripper dressed as a policeman.	On your birthday you turn one year older, and that's no fun no matter who you are. On your un-birthday you gain the right to tell everyone around you that you are one year younger than the age you are actually turning —and that, Divas, is super fun!
...throw a **Bitter Betty Ball.**	It's Valentine's Day and you don't have a date. The good news is that neither do any of your friends. Ask them to get all dolled up in their tackiest gowns and head over to your pad for a glass or three of wine, girl anthem music, and a much-needed vent session about relationships past.
...make it **Christmas in July.**	It's so hot outside, what better way for you and your friends to cool off than to rent an air conditioner, break out the Christmas decorations, and encourage unseasonable gift-giving?

THE EVENT...	ANYONE ELSE WOULD...
Your sister Diva is getting married	...organize a bachelorette party.
You got a pay raise	...take a few close pals out to dinner to celebrate.
Holiday Season	...gather everyone up for a Christmas/Hanukkah/Kwanzaa party.

A SOCIAL DIVA WOULD…	THE DEAL…
…throw a **Diva Funeral.**	Get all your guests to wear black and bring flowers to celebrate the death of their dear Diva's single status.
…throw a **Shoe Shower.**	Now you can finally buy those Manolo Blahnik stilettos. Once you make your lofty purchase, have a coming-out party for your new kicks. Parents-to-be get to have baby showers all the time, so who's to say you can't have a shower to celebrate the newest addition to your high-style footwear family?
…throw a **Bad to Worse Gift Exchange.**	Guests rewrap the worst gift they've received and bring it to the party. Then you all play Pass the Parcel or Lucky Dip until everyone has a different (and probably even worse) gift than what they showed up with.

The Dos and Don'ts of the Guest List

Once you're set on what kind of party you're going to throw, it's time to choose those lucky folks who will comprise the all-important guest list.

When it comes to the right people to invite to your soirée, here are some simple dos and don'ts. Learn them, live them, love them…You'll thank us later when your party is devoid of boring conversationalists and unruly guests.

PARTY TIPS

- **Do** invite your closest circle of friends. You don't want to leave out any of your favorite Diva pals—you *sooo* love them—and you'll also need their help if anything goes awry during your gathering.

- **Don't** invite anyone who has a reputation for being a buzzkill. You don't want your party vibe to come to a screeching halt.

- **Don't** invite a gaggle of women and only two men. (Saucer of milk, table nine! Hellooo!) At your party, you want to keep the ratio of men to women as balanced as possible in order to avoid any cat fights.

- **Do** have a B-list. If you find your guest list is way too big, separate your master list into "A" and "B" lists. If someone on "A" can't make it to your shindig, you can always fill their spot by inviting someone from "B."

- **Don't** divulge to *anyone* the names that make up the B-list—you don't want to hurt someone's feelings.

- **Do** play matchmaker. Feel free to invite two people who might be meant for each other. Introduce them, and then let them be. If by chance they don't get along, they'll have plenty of other people to chitchat with. But if they do indeed dig each other, then you've most certainly done your good Diva deed for the day!

- **Don't** invite anyone who has recently dropped out of Alcoholics Anonymous. These folks have the potential to become "unruly guests," which is something we'll get to in a minute.

- **Do** invite friends and co-workers when the occasion is appropriate. Just make sure you have a fairly even number of people from both groups—you don't want anyone to feel left out in the conversation.

- **Don't** invite the ex-boyfriend of a close Diva pal. We don't care how long you and that particular guy have been friends. In fact, we don't care if he's your brother. It is against Holy Diva Law to put a fellow Diva into a situation like that. Plus, we can almost guarantee that it will cause someone to have a total emotional breakdown, thus ruining your party (i.e., bad karma).

How a Social Diva Deals With an Unruly Guest

If you find yourself presented with an unruly guest (i.e., your neighbor starts chatting up your best friend's boyfriend), your job as Diva hostess is to remove that individual from the party immediately. Think of it as your chance in life to be a bouncer.

If the unruly guest has had too much to drink (which is probably why he or she is so unruly to begin with), call a cab and ask the guest—politely—to take the cab home for a strong cup of coffee and a cold shower.

If the unruly guest continues to be, well, unruly, and simply refuses to leave, only one option is left, Diva, and that is to lock *that person* in the bathroom. We know, we know, it sounds harsh. But it will separate *that person* from the rest of your guests, allow *that person* some time to sober up (or pass out, as the case may be), and if that person feels the need to regurgitate any of the snacks you served, *that person* is close enough to a toilet to avoid a serious mess.

See, Diva? Everybody wins when you lock the unruly guest in the bathroom!

THE BATHROOM ALTERNATIVE

 If you have only one bathroom, usher your drunken guest into a bedroom to sober up. Make sure you put a trash can in the room for any "mishaps" that may occur during the sobering-up process, if you know what we mean.

Feeding the Masses

You always want to have some sort of food available for your party guests, not only to provide padding for the plentiful alcohol you'll be serving but also because the buffet table is an awesome place for guests to strike up conversations with each other.

Designing the Menu

When it comes to what you should serve, it totally depends on what kind of party you're throwing. For example, you wouldn't serve caviar to guests at a barbeque, and you wouldn't offer hamburgers and hot dogs at your annual Oscar party.

It's also important to consider the eatability of the items you plan to serve at your party. Now, we're not saying that you should only serve foods that match the color of your flooring, but it's usually a good idea to stay away from treats that are notoriously messy like drippy pizza rolls, and stick with finger food, which is easy to eat while walking around and chatting.

NIX THE PEANUTS

Did you know that most airlines have stopped serving peanuts on their flights because of the huge number of people who are allergic to them? So, Diva, when designing the menu for your soirée, try to stay away from dishes that include peanuts or peanut oil.

Additionally, it's always a good idea to refrain from serving any food items that contain ingredients many people are allergic to.

To cook or to cater?

Serving only finger foods? Having a barbeque? Inviting only ten people? Then put on your oven mitts, Diva, because it's time to hit the kitchen and start cooking. If the menu you've planned is super-easy to prepare, or if you're inviting a minimal number of guests, it should take you no time at all.

If you're throwing a summertime cookout, your guests will expect to see someone flipping burgers behind the barbie. Grab your tongs and your "Kiss the Cook" apron and assume the position behind your Weber grill. If you're not up to it, grab the nearest male and bribe him to take charge of the charcoal by promising him a dinner on you in the not-so-distant future.

Inviting more than twenty people for a dinner party and you've been known to burn soup? Grab your address book and phone your favorite caterer. Catering companies charge per head, so keep your guest list somewhere between twenty and fifty, and the bill won't be too high. The food will be served on the caterer's platters, eliminating the need to throw a Diva Dish-Washing Party the next day!

If you can't cook, and don't want to shell out big bucks to have someone else cook for you, ask your guests to bring a dish or two. Not only will it save you money, it's guaranteed that there will be something for everyone on your buffet table.

REMEMBER THE VEGANS

 When designing your menu, take into consideration that some of your guests may be vegetarians. Have at least three different food items they can snack on. Social Divas don't discriminate against herbivores!

Cocktails, Anyone?

It's a party, Diva! *Of course* you're serving cocktails! The only question is, which cocktails will fit into your party plan?

If you've invited all your friends to a low-key get-together, stock up on choices of beer. Choose well-known labels, but offer a range of types of beer. For example, alongside the Stella Artois and Grolsch, you could have Boddingtons and Guinness. This mixture of light, medium, and dark should satisfy most tastes.

If you're throwing a more upscale do, provide your guests with the option of red or white wine. In addition, we suggest you mix up a vat of themed cocktails. For example, if you're having a Bitter Betty Ball on Valentine's Day, mix up some chocolate martinis for your guests (garnish the glasses with those cute little Love Heart sweets). If you're having Christmas in July, stir up some eggnog and serve it in a cocktail glass with a tropical umbrella for garnish.

Bitter Betty's Chocolate Martini

1 shot of vodka
2 teaspoons crème de cacao
Splash of cream

Put all the ingredients in a cocktail shaker, add some ice and shake well. Pour into a martini glass, garnish with one or two Love Heart sweets and enjoy!

Providing Proper Glassware

You want to know what drives us *absolutely crazy*? When someone serves us a drink in the incorrect glass. Um, hello? The reason your white wineglasses came in a box labeled "White Wine Glasses" is because they were specifically designed to optimize the flavor of white wine. (Jeez!)

To ensure that you never, ever commit this party faux pas, here is a list of typical glassware and the drinks typically served within them, (pages 40-41).

Get the Right Glass

GLASS	TRADITIONALLY HOLDS…	DRINK SUCH AS…
Cocktail	Traditional martinis, martini cocktails, and any drink ordered "straight up"	Cosmopolitan, Lemon Drop, 007
Collins	Collins variations, sours, and other drinks that are mixed with juice	Tom Collins, Bloody Mary, Whisky Sour
Coupette	Margaritas and margarita variations	Grateful Dead, Cadillac Margarita
Flute	Champagne or drinks mixed with champagne	Mimosa, Bellini
Highball	Drinks mixed with juice or soda water; also used for anything ordered as a "double, on the rocks"	White Russian, Bay Breeze, Jack and Ginger, 7 and 7
Pilsner	Lager beer	Stella Artois, Grolsch
Pint	Any beer	Guinness, Sweetwater, Amstel

GLASS	TRADITIONALLY HOLDS...	DRINK SUCH AS...
Red Wine	Red wine	Cabernet, Merlot, Chianti
Rocks/Old-Fashioned	Chilled shots containing juice, and any spirit ordered "on the rocks" or "short"	Fuzzy Navel, Red Snapper, Black Russian
Schooner	Sherry, port, and straight or chilled liquors	Harvey's, Cockburn's, Cointreau
Shot	Straight or chilled spirits, or mixed shots	Tequila, Alabama Slammer, Flaming Dr. Pepper
Snifter	Straight or mixed brandy	Amaretto Alexander, Nuts and Berries, Blueberry Tea
White Wine	White Wine	Sauvignon Blanc, Pinot Grigio, Chardonnay

COOL AND WHITE

When drinking white wine, it is customary to hold the glass by its stem. Why? Because white wine is traditionally served chilled, and if you were to hold the glass around its bowl, the warmth from your hand would quickly make the wine lose its chill. This is why white-wine glasses have longer stems than red-wine glasses.

Now, That's Entertainment!

When it comes to entertaining your guests, find an act that lends itself to the party you intend to throw.

Do you want people to boogie on down? If so, a DJ is probably your best bet. Just about everyone knows somebody who spins, so ring up your most trusted record slinger and offer him or her a few dollars to play at your party. If you don't know a DJ and can't afford to employ one for the entire night, call an entertainment company and ask if you can hire a DJ to spin at your bash for the first two or three hours. Once the DJ packs up and leaves, you can take over by hooking up your iPod to the stereo system. See, Diva, the hired DJ has already done the hard work for you by setting the mood and the vibe; now all you have to worry about is choosing playlists that follow suit.

Do you want to hold your own sing-a-long session? Hire a live band. Be sure to sample their music beforehand, and request a comprehensive list of every song in their collection to ensure that the music they provide will agree with your theme and guests. Short on cash for a ten-piece band with a killer horn section? Phone your favorite bar and ask if they can recommend some local bands for your get-together.

Do you want loads of silly pictures of your girlfriends? Diva, you need to hire yourself a male stripper! Yes, it sounds a little cheesy, but when one of these guys shows up at your door and embarrasses the pants off your friend (pun intended) at her Diva Funeral (see pages 30-31), you'll be thanking us. Plus, think about the future: What's more fun than reminiscing over some hilarious photos of your best friend attempting to put a dollar in a guy's electric yellow thong using only her feet? Umm, *nothing*, that's what!

SPEAKING OF SILLY PICTURES...

When throwing a party at your posh pad, it's usually a good idea to employ one of your pals to be the Official Party Photographer. Make sure you ask someone who is good with a camera (i.e., doesn't have a reputation for cutting off people's heads), and have them snap away at all the fun happenings. If no one in your posse really fits the bill, you could always hire a pro—your own personal paparazzo!

The Elusive Goodie Bag

It's a fact of life, Diva...people *love* gifts! So when you're planning your party, be sure to include goodie bags in your budget.

But before you go and overdraw your bank account, remember that your guests do not expect your swag to rival that given out at the Sundance Film Festival: "fabulous" doesn't have to cost a lot of moola. When choosing your goodie bag contents, pick items that coordinate with your party theme and, if your party is co-ed, are appropriate for both men and women.

For example, if you're throwing a Swingin' Sushi Dinner Party, go online to:

www.greatorientalgifts.com or **www.culturalintrigue.com** and get some pretty gift bags ($1.99) to fill with the following:

- Pair of cute chopsticks (make sure they're reusable) $.99

- Pack of Japanese incense sticks $2.49

- Bar of prettily wrapped sandalwood soap $2.39

- Painted folding fan $2.98

Do the math, Divas! That's four adorable and totally usable gifts for your guests at a cost of less than $11.00 per person.

Watch It All Come Together

Remember, Diva, that when it comes to throwing a soirée of your own, the most important thing to do is to stay calm. Don't stress yourself out over minute details that, in the end, don't really mean anything to your guests. Just make sure that everyone has yummy food in their tummies, drinks in hand, and interesting people to mingle with, and your job as the Diva-licious hostess with the mostest is complete.

Now all you have to do is sit back, relax, and watch those hostess gifts (see page 105) roll on in!

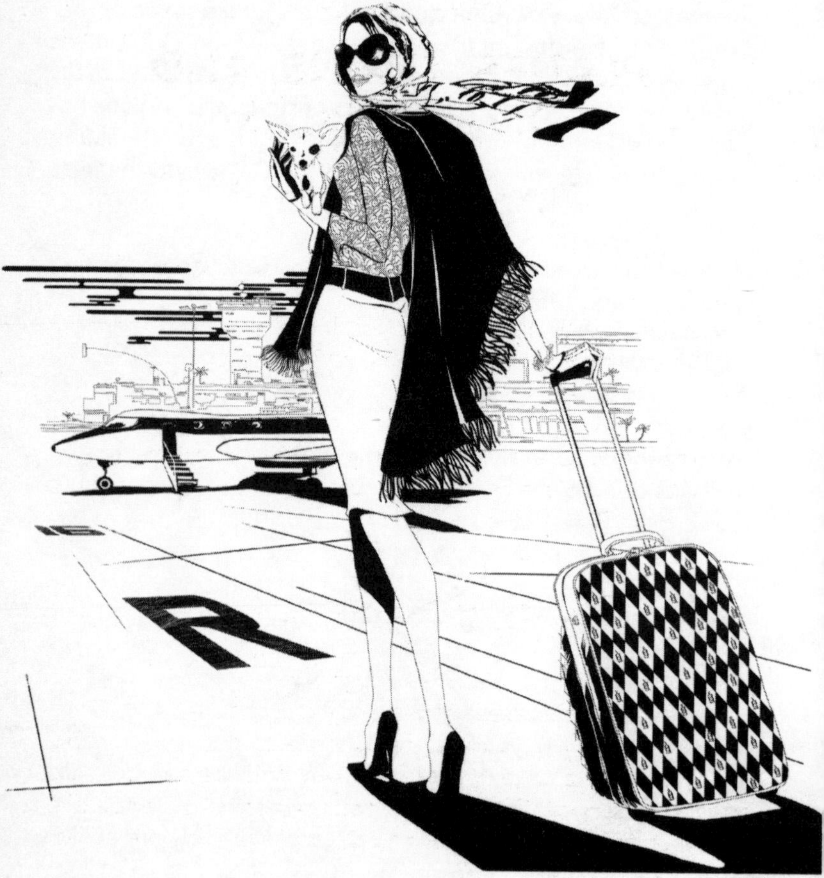

Chapter Three

PLANES, TRAINS, AND DIVA-MOBILES

How a Social Diva Travels

If you are tired of partying at chez Diva, or in your home city for that matter, why not hop on a plane and get out of town for a swinging soirée?

So whether you're flying with the masses or enjoying the delights of a private jet, here are some tips to make traveling much more Diva-esque.

Getting to the Airport

Know your timing, Diva! These days it doesn't do a Diva any good to rush. This causes stress, and that produces frown lines. Make sure you give yourself enough time to get to the airport. Are you driving or taking a taxi? Wait...did we say taxi? We meant car service. The cars are much nicer and more reliable, and that leaves one less thing to chance. Plus, you *are* a Diva, after all!

Check in or Carry On?

You know the drill: upon arriving at the airport, you present your ticket and passport at check-in and then have to decide what to do with your bag. Clearly, sticking with carry-on luggage saves precious time later. After all, who wants to stand there watching and waiting for baggage for a half hour or more? We'd rather be en route to our first martini at the hotel bar. Plus, what if (gasp) your luggage gets lost? How are you going to replace that vintage Prada dress for your evening out? Being a Diva means taking everything that is irreplaceable in your carry-on bag. And we mean *everything*.

Three carry-on must-haves

1. iPod: Can we say baby crying or loudmouths standing in line for the toilet? Putting headphones on not only blocks out the entire world but also serves as a "do not talk to me" sign to any chatty type sitting next to you.

2. Reading material: Beyond merely entertaining, a book or magazine is also handy as an alternative means of zoning out the above-mentioned kids and chatty travelers.

3. Cell phone charger: Never, ever, *ever* put this in your checked-in bag. Your cell phone is what is going to save you from the rest of the airport craziness if your flight is delayed. You can use that extra time to catch up with people, check your e-mail, or rearrange your schedule. You do not *ever* want a dead phone when traveling.

When a trip is for over five days or you're going to a cold climate you just might have to check a heavier bag before boarding. After all, a Social Diva needs to pack more: at least one evening dress (just in case) and extra layers for warmth. If you find yourself in this position, checking in at a self-service kiosk speeds up travel time.

Getting an Upgrade

Upgrading your seat can depend on many different factors, including how much you fly, when you are flying, and who you get as your ticket agent. Here are a few guidelines for securing a first-class seat:

- *Travel off-peak.* The more empty seats, the better your chances of getting moved up.

- *When booking, ask what type of ticket you are buying.* Some tickets are not upgradeable, while others require an extra fee to upgrade. Know these restrictions—they will come into play if you want to change your ticket.

- *Once you're at the airport, ask for an upgrade.* You can't get what you don't ask for, and airlines are rarely going to offer.

Secure and Safe

We know that security checks are time-consuming and a little embarrassing—who wants the whole world to see her toiletries?

But fear not: no one really looks, and the inspectors are just as agitated as you are about the process. Getting through security at least for now, means placing all of your carry-on liquids—none over 3 oz.—in a single, transparent, resealable plastic bag, removing your laptop from your bag for a separate screening, and taking off your shoes, belt and anything else that might make the dreaded "beep" when you pass through the detector. While going through this process, try to smile. The security people will appreciate it, and the procedure becomes more tolerable for everyone.

BAG YOUR BLING!

Set apart all the jewelry you want to wear with your traveling outfit. Instead of putting it on, pack it in a small cosmetics bag and tuck it away in your handbag. The less bling you have on in the security line, the less chance you have of being stopped. You can adorn yourself later, once you reach the departure lounge.

The Dreaded Delay

Divas, it is well known that afternoon and evening flights are always delayed. If you have same-day evening plans, do not, we repeat, *do not* take an afternoon flight. If you do, you will inevitably show up more than fashionably late, if you show up at all. Trust us, we've been there.

Case in point: Peg was headed to Miami for the MTV Awards, and all the available flights were canceled or delayed. Her only viable option was to fly out at the crack of dawn next day.

However, not wanting to miss a thing, Peg nixed the idea of departing bright and early, and finagled her way on to the very last flight to Miami. *Big mistake.*

When she finally arrived, she had totally missed that night's party, and all the added stress of getting on that flight was a total energy-waster. Looking back, she would rather have flown out first thing in the morning, first class of course, and started fresh.

So, what if your flight is (gasp!) delayed? Well, it depends on how long. Once you know, there are various things you can do to optimize your Diva time.

Less than 45 minutes: Grab an extra-trashy magazine. You needed to catch up on the antics of TomKat, LiLo, and the Beckhams anyway.

Up to two hours: If you are not already an elite member of your airline, consider signing up. That way you could be chilling in the Admiral's Club, or similar, waiting for your flight. As Divas prefer first class to economy, we also lean toward elite rooms over terminals. Plus, the ticketing agents are undoubtedly friendlier.

Over two hours: Soak up the latest bestseller—which will also help you be well versed for cocktail party chatter. Speaking of soaking, find out if there is a spa in the airport—you might as well spend your delay time on something useful, like getting pampered.

Go Private

Ignorance is bliss, Divas, because once you fly by private plane, you will have an extremely hard time going back to commercial airways. In the world of private travel people handle your bags for you and security is much easier. You pretty much have a personal assistant throughout your flying experience. If you get the opportunity, and have never flown private before, go with the flow and take cues from those around you. After all, you *are* a Social Diva, and you don't want anyone to know this isn't how you fly all the time. For the most part the rule of thumb is just follow, watch, and smile.

Planning Your Trip

Where can a Diva go? Anywhere she wants! The options are limitless. Tired of the cold weather? Are you ready for some city action? Are the snowcaps calling your name? Or did you just get a brilliant last-minute invitation to the Cannes Film Festival? The choice is yours as a Social Diva who has lots of invitations.

IF I FORGET SOMETHING, I CAN JUST BUY IT THERE…

This attitude is a waste of your precious time. You're probably not familiar with the geography of your destination, so you might spend hours looking for cute flip-flops when you could be taking a disco nap* to revive you from your long journey and prepare you for some stress-free fun.

A light slumber that lasts no more than one hour, taken in order to refresh the body and mind in preparation for the late night ahead.

What to Pack

There's no doubt about it—packing is an art, and few of us have mastered it. The idea is to travel light, taking items that can be mixed and matched so that you can be the best-dressed Diva whatever the circumstances. A simple cotton dress, for example, is a great cover-up on the beach, and, with the addition of sparkly sandals, can easily make the transition to a restaurant for lunch. In the evening, wear it with heels for a night on the town.

LONG BEACH WEEKEND CHECKLIST
• Underwear, including thongs and a strapless bra

• Negligee

• Two pairs of jeans (wear one pair on the plane)

• Two dresses (preferably one solid black, and one in whatever color or print you look most fabulous)

• At least two bikinis (so that you never have to put on a wet one; include a plastic bag for them if not totally dry when it's time to hop the plane home)

• Sparkly flip-flops/sandals (kitten heels optional)

• High heels (neutral enough to match your dresses; if you have room, pack two pairs, but leave space for purchases you make on your trip)

- Accessories (dangly earrings a must—they can turn any outfit from day to night)

- Cute little top (for casual wear with jeans)

- Kaftan (preferably white with long sleeves, to cover up after swimming or sunbathing. Avoid black—it absorbs the heat and you'll look like a tourist. And Social Divas are not tourists…they are *travelers*)

- Large shades (essential to protect your eyes and the delicate skin around them)

- Cosmetics (your regular arsenal, plus sunblock for body, face, and lips; a little spritzer for freshening up when you see a cute man; aloe, just in case you turn red; and a little bronzer to accent your newly sun-kissed face)

At this point it's important to note that Social Divas should always be prepared for a surprise invitation. A girlfriend staying with Peg in Miami received a last-minute invitation to a party in Aspen. Luckily, the contents of her bag for Miami included a gorgeous evening dress and a fur wrap. Just goes to show you, Diva, you must be prepared!

SOMETHING IN COMMON

When packing for a trip, choose garments that have a common color scheme, or at least complement each other. This makes it easier to minimize the number of accessories and shoes you'll have to squeeze into your bag.

Snow Know-How

Having explained how to pack for the beach, it's high time we showed you how to pack for the chill. And, prepare yourselves, this time it is necessary to check your bag at the airport.

SKI TRIP CHECKLIST

- Sweaters (pack these first, laid out flat at the bottom of your suitcase; this will save space and make them less likely to wrinkle)

- Ski pants and jacket (more adaptable than all-in-one suit)

- Jeans (nothing says "casual winter weekend" quite like denim)

- T-shirts to relax in for day or to dress up for a night at the bar

- Funky party top (for when you want to dress up your tee and jeans)

- Silk undergarments, leggings (useful as both under and outer wear), and plenty of socks

- Fabulous snow boots (a great fashion statement après-ski, though they don't provide much traction for walking)

- Walking boots (to keep you on your feet rather than your tush)

- Gloves (both ski and knit)

- Goggles

SEND AHEAD

If you're going on a long trip that requires lots of bulky clothes, or you're simply notorious for overpacking, ship your luggage ahead so that it's waiting when you arrive.

As you already know, Diva, you have to have the ski-garb basics for the slopes. Layering is terrific for warmth and comfort in the great outdoors, and adapts marvelously to après-ski. Just strip off the top layers and you're no longer bulky. You might want to freshen up a bit, considering you've been on the slopes all day. Luckily, it's easy to stash stuff in those handy zippered pockets on your ski gear. Necessities include Chapstick for slope duty, lip gloss for a post-ski shimmer (which can also be used as blush in a pinch), and mascara. Five minutes in front of a mirror and voilà!—you'll be looking Diva-tastic!

If you want to check yourself out pre-ladies' room, carry a tiny mirror, or take a peek at your appearance on the shiny surface of your cell, your goggles, or even your iPod.

In the evening, most ski resorts are pretty casual. Typically, you can get away with jeans and a simple top. If more glamour is needed, accessories go a long way. For example, in Aspen turquoise and a cowboy hat complete the "it" look. You sport those, Diva, and you are in fashion like a local. Don't worry, we know the cowboy hat is hard to fit in that carry-on bag, so either wear it on the plane or buy it when you arrive. (Trendy items of the moment will be on sale in every shop, so you'll easily be able to find what you need.)

In the cold weather do what your mother always said (you don't have to tell her she was right) and wear your coat, scarf, gloves, and hat (if it doesn't mess up your hair) to stay warm in sub-zero temps. Social Divas do not want to catch cold. We don't have time to waste when there's partying to be done!

City Smarts

If you are a country-living or a car-driving Diva, visiting a city such as New York, Paris, London, or Milan for the first time can be a shock. The fact is, Diva, you are going to be doing a lot of walking, so your choice of footwear is the most important aspect of your packing extravaganza. Pack at least three or four pairs of shoes. This is not the time to break in those new heels (unless you're hitting the clubs, where you know you'll be taking a taxi anyway).

Sightseeing, shopping, dining, and clubbing are all top of the to-do list while in the bright lights. As a Social Diva, you must be prepared and plan your packing choices wisely.

THE DISCREET SHOE SWAP

If you plan on hitting the road, take a tip from city-dwellers and engage in what they call the "shoe swap." Wear your compactable comfy walking shoes when you leave home, and tuck your uber-fabulous shoes into your big, slouchy bag. When you are a short distance away from your destination, swap the shoes you have on your feet with the shoes in your bag. Now you can work those wedges like you've been in them all day, and no one will be the wiser!

If you don't have a big slouchy bag, you can buy one cheaply on virtually any street corner in the city. Pick something in a solid color and a decent material (not a blatant knock-off with a bad logo). If you choose wisely, there's a good chance that people will think it is the next "It" bag. Sooo Diva!

CITY BREAK CHECKLIST

- Basics: undies, nightclothes, stockings, and socks
- Two pairs of jeans (wear one on the plane and pack the other)
- Flat shoes (essential for walking around and negotiating cobble-stoned streets)
- Two pairs of heels (you never know when you're going to get new blisters—even the most comfortable heels become painful after pounding the pavement for hours)
- Jacket (choose according to destination and time of year; if you live in a cold part of the world and are going somewhere warm, tough it out and wear something lightweight to the airport—gives you one more item to mix and match, and you won't have to deal with a bulky garment)
- Large day bag
- Small evening bag

Romantic Weekend

A man asks you to go out of town with him. All you need to do is agree on the date and he will handle the rest.

Now what on earth do you pack?

First things first: figure out what kind of bag you'll tote. We suggest a small carry-on bag. When you arrive he'll think, "Wow, she is totally low maintenance! Look at how she's fit everything she needs to look fabulous in that little bag." This is when you give a little smile and say, "Oh, I only needed a couple of things." Let him wonder what those things are and at the same time be amazed by how Diva-licious you look. Plus, you'll feel empowered by your supreme packing skills.

If he plans to take you to a black-tie event, he'll probably mention it in advance, since we know, as a Social Diva, you always date gentlemen. In that case, you'll know to pack that Gucci number.

As for everyday attire, look back at the lists in "What to Pack" starting on page 53 to see what's recommended for different types of destinations, and be certain to pack the following extras for those "just in case" events:

ROMANTIC WEEKEND CHECKLIST
• Little black dress (a Diva can always fit one into her suitcase, and it's a necessity for a night on the town with Mr. Right or Mr. Right Now)

- Small evening bag (one that can hold a few essentials)

- Your naughtiest little number (for later, daaahhling).

Where to Stay

It's wonderful to be whisked away for the weekend, but what happens when you're organizing things yourself? If you are a Diva on a budget, it's always nice to get the use of your friend's fab beach house in the Hamptons or ski lodge in the French Alps. Just make sure you always treat the place as your own most cherished possession. Social Divas do not mistreat their friend's things, especially not their property, so if you tend toward breaking things, or not doing the dishes, we suggest you stay in a hotel instead. There are many stylish and affordable places you can stay (and room service is just a phone call away).

We suggest going the boutique hotel route. Boutique hotels, for example, are sooo diva. They attract those people who want something a little unique, hip, and fun. Just like you. There are lots of choices for these hotels, one great spot to find them is Tablet Hotels (**www.TabletHotels.com**). They scout and review the most unique hotels across the world and feature gorgeous photos of all their finds. Their website offers a super-easy reservation service and always features Diva-worthy exclusive specials.

Feel more comfortable at a chain, or you're working your loyalty miles? W Hotels are our fave. Any hotel that has a button marked "Whatever Whenever" on its room phones (and really means it) is, well—priceless!

If you are a frequent traveler, you are eligible for loyalty rewards, or are savvy enough to work your Diva magic and get an upgrade. The secret is in knowing how to ask. When booking, ask lots of questions about your options. Inquire about what size rooms they have, and which side of the hotel is quieter (the last thing you want is a room over a street full of party-goers, car horns, or booming nightclub music). Also, make sure you request a non-smoking room (unless, of course, you are a smoker).

Upon arrival, ask at the reception desk about upgrade options. Be incredibly nice—the nicer you are, the greater the likelihood of getting an upgrade. Try something as simple as, "Is there any chance I can get upgraded?" Maintain a huge smile on your face—it goes a looong way. The worst that can happen is that they'll say no. On the other hand, the best-case scenario will find you in the Presidential Suite, just as a true Social Diva should be!

ALTERNATIVE USES FOR HOTEL TOILETRIES
Hair conditioner: Use this as shaving cream to keep you smooth between waxes. It's moisturizing, smells yummy, and you'll save space in your bag.

Shower cap: Can be used to wrap up a leaky bottle or a damp bathing suit when you're packing for the trip home.

Soap: Use to remove any stains your garments might have suffered the night before.

Steam: OK, not strictly a toiletry, but very useful nonetheless. Just hang your garments in the bathroom while you shower to straighten out any wrinkles from the trip.

Now that you know how to handle a Social Diva getaway, you can plan your next trip out of town confident that you will be fully prepared. Bon voyage!

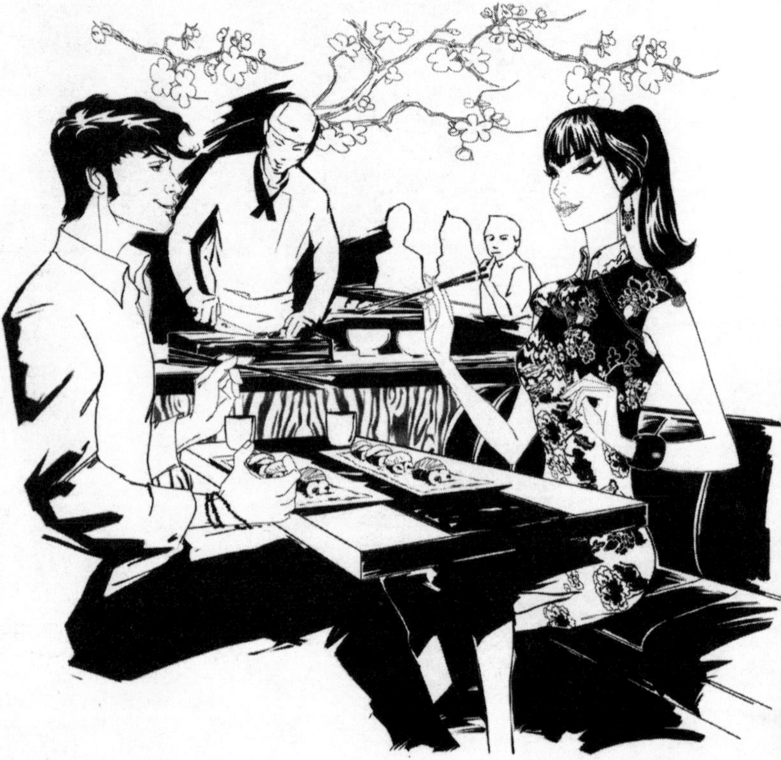

Chapter Four

THOSE CHOPSTICKS MAKE YOUR BUTT LOOK FABULOUS

How a Social Diva Does Dining Out

You walk into a restaurant and the hostess greets you with a smile. She escorts you straight to your table (there's no wait for Divas) or to the restaurant's hip, swanky bar for a pre-dinner cocktail. The vibe is right, the lighting makes you look your most fabulous, the music is perfect for the mood, and everyone looks amazing. And Divas, all this is happening before you have even tried the food. You sit down and the service is perfect; they come by enough but not too much. And naturally, everything is yummy! This is what we call Diva-worthy dining.

Where to Go

When choosing a dining destination, first things first. Decide what type of food you're yearning for: sushi, Italian, Thai, French, Chinese—so many choices for just one meal! In addition to your own taste bud preferences, pick a spot with an atmosphere that suits the occasion. Getting together with friends? Dining alone? An intimate date? (If it's the last option, let's hope your date picks the place. However, he might ask you to suggest a place, so it's good to be prepared with a few trendy ideas.)

Need to find out what the best restaurants in town are? Word of mouth recommendations are your best bet, so listen to your friends. After all, you probably enjoy the same food and ambience. Another option is to peruse the local paper or read reviews on websites like Chowhound or Yelp. When choosing this option, find a reviewer who has similar tastes to your own. You can only do this by trial and error, so if you visit a restaurant and find the review way off the mark, you'll know not to trust that critic next time you're choosing a spot.

Getting a Table

"Do you have a reservation?" Those five little words can make or break your evening. Since waiting sucks, be prepared. And by "prepared" we mean call in advance or know how to sweet-talk the maître d'.

If you know where you want to go and the restaurant is on the Hot-Right-Now List, you should already know that getting a table at a prime-dine time is going to be difficult.

PRIME DINE TIMES

 Thursday, Friday, or Saturday nights between 7:30 p.m. and 9:30 p.m. (a little earlier if the eatery is in the suburbs) are what we call prime dine times.

The sooner you know your plans, the better to call the restaurant. But never call during the lunch or dinner rush. If the place is happening, they won't be as flexible. It's best to call around three or four in the afternoon, when things are slow. Ask for your prime-dine-time reservation. If you can't get what you want, ask what's available—there might be a time just as good for you and your friends, and sometimes it's no sacrifice to modify your plans. If you're offered ridiculous options, such as the early bird special (not in your vocabulary? We didn't think so), then it is time to get creative.

Sometimes it helps if you mention that it is a very special occasion, for instance, the "birthday girl" is so looking forward to dining there. Flattery can also ease your way to a table. Mention the fabulous write-up they received in the newspaper, and that you simply can't wait to see what all the fuss is about. If all else fails (and you aren't best friends with a publicist), call up and say you are Dita Von Diva from Say No More Public Relations, and that you have a "very special" VIP coming in on Saturday night. You won't give them the name because you can't let it to get out to the press (paparazzi are just soooo 1995). This usually does the trick and, to be honest, the person who takes the booking will most likely not be on duty the night of your dinner. But if you do get caught, you can always claim you're the star on the latest reality TV series, or the daughter of someone famous (no one knows what those people look like anyway).

Getting In Without a Reservation

It pays to have a friendly face for service industry people. Smiling always works well. Having worked in restaurants, we know that the warm and friendly person will always be favored over the trout-lipped bitch who acts like she's entitled to a table because of her bank balance. Social Divas are never rude or condescending; they are always fabulous and friendly.

Waiting time
Here's a handy guide to working out whether to keep waiting for a table or hit the road.

Less than thirty minutes: Wait it out. You wanted to scope out the uber-chic bar scene anyway, so that is perfecto!

Forty-five minutes to one and a half hours: This is a gray area; it's possible you could be waiting all night, or the restaurant is way overbooked and they are trying to scare you off with an obscene waiting time. Have one drink, then check in with the hostess and see if the wait it is reasonable yet or you should jet.

One and a half to three hours: Get out of there! Three hours in Diva Time is the equivalent to two fabulous spa treatments.

Hit the Stool

If the wait is too long, or if you're super-hungry, find out if you can have your dinner at the bar. After all, this particular area of the restaurant is usually more entertaining, offers better service, and is more social than a table. Think about it, Diva, the bartender waits on you, so he is always right there when you need him and, typically, he wants to chat (given that most of his conversations consist of people calling out drink orders and moving on). As a result of your friendliness, he might even buy you a drink or give you dessert on the house. Now what is more Diva than that?

The Last Resort

If you absolutely must have the comforts of a table (and don't want to try your luck at the next packed restaurant or, even worse, eat "street meat" from a hotdog vendor), do it like a dude and slip the maître d' a fifty. You will be seated next. Period.

Opening Night

Peg says that opening night is her favorite holiday (seriously, she says that out loud). Opening night is generally a preview of the city's latest dining experience. "Everyone" is there, everything is new, and the vibe is just right. However, this is not the best night to seriously try the food. Generally, there are small plates of canapés going around, and you barely get a nibble in between cocktails. Do yourself a favor and eat beforehand. Tell the chef/owner/PR person that everything was fabulous, and come back in a week or so to try the eats.

How to get invited to these soirées? Research the restaurant PR firms in your city (there are usually just a few that specialize in restaurants) and get on their mailing lists. They need Social Diva hipsters like you to attend their restaurant openings just as badly as they need the press. It makes them look good to have your fabulous self there. Bonus: you get to chat with the head honchos at the venue and this will be gold in the future with the business of getting a table.

Table for One

You open your fridge and you see condiments, Champagne, and some too-old-to-be-edible leftovers. You think about having a cocktail dinner, but then again, you're starving. Order takeout? Boring. Hit the supermarket? We don't think so! Or do you (gasp) go out and eat by yourself?

Though it can be a little scary, think of dining solo as an opportunity to meet new people. Or think about it as a way to give yourself some downtime. Really, how many *more* times do you have to listen to your always available gal pal talk about her "mixed messages" boyfriend who is never going to change his ways? So whether you want to meet someone new or you just want a quiet, leave-me-alone kind of meal, here are some tips for a stellar singular dining experience.

Take a meeting
When dining alone, it is always much easier to meet others (provided you want to) if you eat at the bar. Let's face it, it *is* a bar! People go there to socialize. Plus, you might get a cute

bartender to wait on you—bonus! Meeting people is easier than you might think. A couple of nonverbal cues that signify you are open for conversation should do the trick. Sit up and back, make eye contact, and, of course, smile, Diva!

If you tend to get uncomfortable when by yourself, don't worry—it only lasts about twenty minutes (which is equivalent to two martinis). Once you're relaxed, you'll meet people and get your groove on. Time will fly when you're with your newfound friends, and next thing you know you may wind up at a hot after-party wondering why you ever considered a solo dinner in the first place. Indeed, you might never want to go out with your own friends again! But, you may be asking, how will I entertain myself for those twenty minutes? Well, with props, of course!

RESTAURANT PROPS

Book: You can easily pass the time with a book, plus it is easier to manage than a newspaper and can be easily tucked away in your bag once the opportunity to chat with new people presents itself.

Cell phone: No, it is not for talking! In this situation the phone is for texting and e-mails only. Warning: they don't call them CrackBerrys for nothing. Don't get sucked into working all night on this little device; it has the addictive qualities to tie you up until dessert. Just remember, Diva, this is your social time, so use the phone as a prop to get over the uncomfortable feeling-alone hump.

Notebook: Rewrite your to-do list for the next day, write your wish list of the top seven things you want to accomplish, or scribble "I ♥ Jake Ryan" a million times over! You'll get some Diva quiet time, and others will think you are a reviewer from a hot gourmet magazine.

Take some personal time

If you really want some quality Diva downtime, and still want to have a nice meal out, this can be managed with strategic seating. Sitting at a table or in a booth generally provides an invisible barrier to the world around you. At a table, sitting with your back to the restaurant helps. Tell the maître d' you would like a quiet table in the back because, after such a full day of shooting, you just can't imagine signing another autograph. Well, you might get a little attention and stares from the wait staff if you say that, but hey, you might also get a free drink and meet the chef. Nothing wrong with that!

Take your time perusing the menu and wait to hear about the specials before making your final decision. Typically, the specials are more interesting and imaginative than the standard dishes.

Not familiar with an item on the menu? Don't be shy, Diva. Ask! You're the one who has to eat it, so make certain it is something you can fully enjoy.

Not sure what you want? Again, ask! Get some recommendations from your server. But Divas beware: pay attention not only to what the server suggests, but also to how he answers. For example, if he says, "Tonight's pear tart with cream is simply to die for," then go for it. If he says, "Well, I'm not a chocolate person, but the mousse with macaroon is OK," dismiss the suggestion entirely. After all, who isn't a chocolate person? Their taste buds are obviously as dead as the shoulder-pad trend!

Cocktails anyone?

Naturally, your choice of drink depends on your mood for the evening. Cocktails are always a fabulous option. Order something you can sip on for a while (you don't want to be smashed before your food arrives). Having trouble picking a cocktail? Try a Social Diva-tini! Here's the recipe to relay to your server:

Social Diva-tini

Two shots of Stolichnaya raspberry vodka
Splash of Sprite

Put the ingredients in a cocktail shaker with some ice and shake well. Strain into a traditional martini glass, garnish with a lemon twist—and enjoy!

Wine, they say, is meant to be savored with a meal (who are "they" anyway?). The rules of yesteryear state that white wines should be served with fish and poultry, reds with meat and cheese. These days, it is not only acceptable but encouraged to throw out the rules and order either. A pro server will be able to guide you on which bottle will work with your order and your particular tastes. If you want to look like a real aficionado, ask if the restaurant has a sommelier—a wine professional who can talk you through every bottle on the list and make recommendations that will best complement your meal. If you are with a gentleman, he should taste the wine first, and don't be embarrassed if he rejects it for being corked (having a musty, acrid smell and taste). If you are with girlfriends, take the lead and offer to taste the wine—it prevents any embarrassment at the table in front of the server, and means that you look like you're in control and know what you're doing—very Diva indeed!

CHEERS!

Legend has it that clinking glasses was once part of a ritual in which the host tasted the wine first to show that it was safe to drink (i.e., no one had laced it with poison). Urban legend, however, of late says that when you clink you should look each participating person in the eye, otherwise you'll have seven years of bad sex. If you ever offer either of us a "Cheers," we'll certainly look you straight in the eye—after all, Divas aren't ones to test tales of legendary bad luck!

Indulge...it's what Divas do!

You only have one life, Diva, so enjoy it. If you have room for dessert, and you feel that special warm chocolate fondant cake calling your name, order it. And the espresso too! Why deprive yourself? You are, after all, a Social Diva—and you can always spend twenty extra minutes on the treadmill later...

IMPROMPTU GATHERING

Want an inspired alternative to dining alone? Call some of your friends then contact your favorite takeout restaurant and order lots of different items for everyone to share. It's loads of fun and you get to try things you probably wouldn't have ordered just for yourself.

Paying the Bill

Who foots the bill, and how, depends on who you are dining with.

Out with friends? Split it evenly. If one person had much more food or wine, they should offer to pay extra, but if they don't let it go: this is not something worth getting stressed over. Just keep it simple. Divide the total bill by the number of friends you're with and make sure you round up. Divas never get out their calculators!

On a first date? Our mothers always told us that the man should pay. As women of the millennium, however, we Divas abide by the you-ask, you-pay rule. This simply states that whichever party invited the other should foot the bill. If the date was a disaster and the guy was a loser, pay your share of the bill and leave him with the rest. Don't give him the opportunity of complaining to his friends the next day that he dropped a chunk of change on a bad date.

On a second or third date? Typically, he'll pay up, but Divas always portray an air of independence, so when the bill arrives, reach for your wallet. Nine times out of ten, he'll stop you before you can even pull out your credit card.

Most important, if anyone pays for your meal, express your gratitude—either verbally or with a thank-you note. It's polite, and it almost guarantees that your next meal will end the same way.

Tipping: Not Just a City in China

When it's time to tip, figure 20 percent of the total bill. The easiest and quickest way to do this is to take the first two digits of the total amount and double them after rounding up (i.e., if the bill is $52.80 then round up to 53 and then double equaling a $10.60 tip, which you'd round up, to $11). If you still can't figure it out, that is what cell phone calculators are for, but please pretend you are texting not pulling out the calculator and being cheap.

Nowadays, any tip less than 20 percent is simply cheap and tasteless, unless, of course, the service from your waiter was unacceptable. Let's repeat: *If the service from your waiter was unacceptable.* Service from your waiter has nothing to do with the quality of the food or the hostess's attitude problem! If you've never worked tables before, it's important to know that waiters and waitresses do not make an hourly wage, they work for tips only. How would you feel if you weren't paid for two hours of work because the receptionist at your office kept a client on hold for too long? Yeah, we wouldn't be happy about it either. Plus, most of the time, your server is a college student trying to make ends meet until they graduate. Bottom line: Please give your servers a break and tip them well.

HOLIDAY CHEER

Be generous and throw in a bit extra for your server around Christmas time. It always feels good to play Santa, and it will make their day!

RESTAURANT ETIQUETTE

- If you are dining with a gentleman, always take the inside seat so that your back is to the wall and his back is to the room.

- If you are with a mixed group, ladies sit down first.

- Wait for everyone's dish to arrive before you start eating. However, if the others urge you to start before it gets cold, feel free to dig in.

- If you are with a date and in mid-story when the food arrives at your table, it is polite to tell him he may go ahead and start eating while you finish your tale before your first bite.

Now that you are well versed in finding and enjoying the most exquisite dining hotspots, you can concentrate on more important things…such as what to wear. *Bon appetit!*

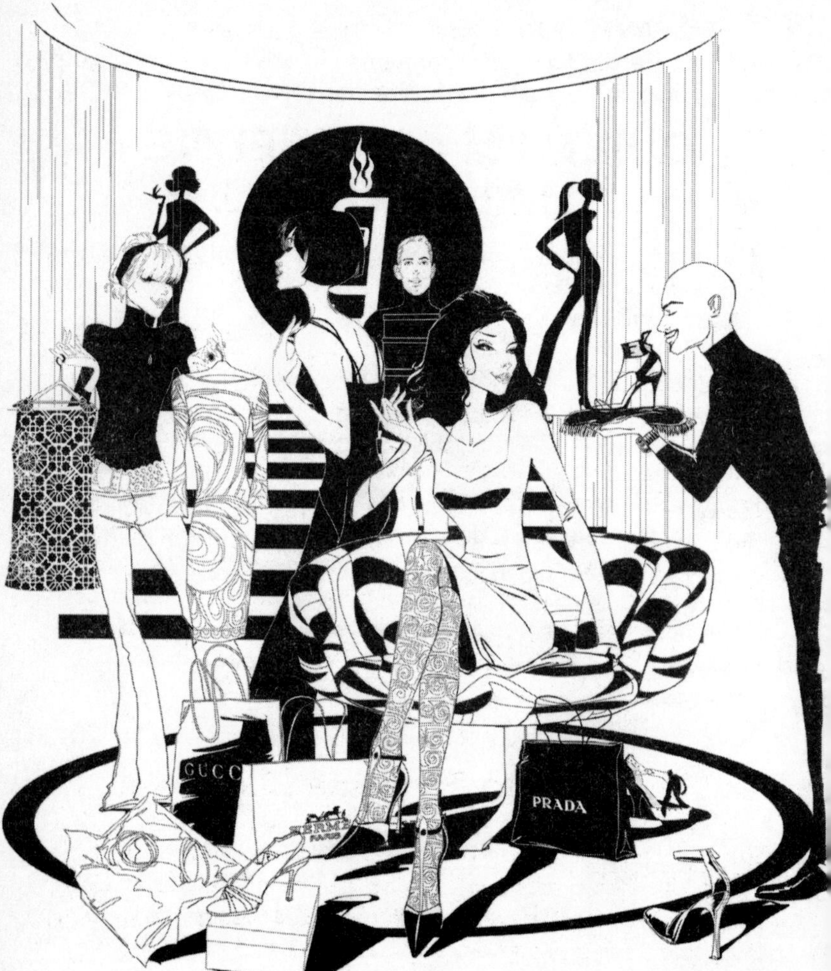
GUCC
PRADA

Chapter Five

QUIET! I'M CHANNELING EMILIO PUCCI!

How a Social Diva Shops

Shopping…it's a Social Diva's favorite pastime. No single activity in the world is as therapeutic, empowering, or fun as hitting your favorite stores to scoop up some utterly fabulous finds. Unfortunately, the busy social schedule that comes with being a Diva sometimes results in a shortage of shopping time. To rectify this problem, we've come up with a few different strategies for efficient and effective shopping (because a Diva simply must be the best-dressed female at every shindig, regardless of her time-management situation!).

How to Shop the Mall

The mall can be a dangerous place for a Diva: children crying, old folks walking as slowly as possible, sales assistants who despise their jobs (and their customers, for that matter). For a Diva, this adds up to a very big headache and an emergency spa visit. Now, before those horrible memories of holiday sale-time madness prevent you from ever stepping foot inside one of these shopping meccas again, why not try our Diva guidelines for successful mall shopping.

KEEP A FASHION NOTEBOOK

Ever notice how at least twice a week you say to yourself, "I really wish I had a pair of red sling-backs to go with these pants/skirt/jeans/etc.," but no matter how many shopping trips you go on, you never remember to look for them? We know we do! From now on, keep a notepad and pen near your closet so that when a red sling-back moment occurs, you can write down "red slingbacks." Now all you have to do is remember to toss the notepad in your bag the next time you go shopping.

When to Go

When planning a trip to the mall, it's necessary to take several different factors into account—namely, time of year, day of week, and time of day.

First rule of mall shopping: you do not talk about mall shopping (sorry, we just had to throw in a *Fight Club* reference here because we ♥ Brad Pitt). Second rule of mall shopping: Never go during the buildup to Christmas. We mean it, Diva! If you need to purchase gifts from the mall, you'd better have that item in your possession by December 1. We know it sounds crazy, but you'll thank us for it by December 2! Those shopping crowds are not to be trifled with; they have worse tempers than an angry mob at an SEC college football game.

The best time of year to go to the mall is when people are taking their summer vacations. Memorial Day is a good bet because everyone is too busy heading for beaches, lakes, and pools to be taking advantage of the huge department store sales. And don't forget to take advantage of major events, such as the Super Bowl or World Series. Stores are deserted because most people are glued to the television.

Once you've determined the appropriate season or holiday for mall shopping, you must decide on a day of the week. Our Diva shopping spies tell us that deliveries of new merchandise to retail outlets tend to happen on Tuesdays—so use this knowledge to get your manicured hands on the new stuff before the masses catch wind of it.

In terms of hours, the best time to visit the mall is between 9:00 a.m. and midday. During this brief period office workers are stuck at their desks, children are safely tucked away in their classrooms, and sales assistants are not yet feeling cranky. *Do not* visit any mall between 3:00 and 6:00 in the afternoon. This is when parents descend with ill-tempered children, and teenagers loaf about looking for action.

QUIET TIME

 The quietest shopping days are typically Monday and Tuesday. If it's raining, shopping centers are much busier.

How to get in (and get the hell out)

Considering how busy (and irritating) malls can be, most of us just want to get in and out of them as quickly as possible. The best way to do this, Divas, is to plan your trip with exacting attention to detail.

To ensure shopping efficiency, you must first familiarize yourself with the basic layout of your local mall. Then make a list of which stores you need to hit and what you need from each of them. Comparing your list to the mall layout, you will then come up with a game plan that will direct you to the proper place to park, and the order in which to visit your chosen shops.

For example, let's say you need to visit Nordstrom for some new jeans, Saks for a hip "it" bag, and Victoria's Secret for some cute little underthings for a weekend with your new George Clooney look-alike. First, assess which of the stores is closest to a mall entrance. Park in the area directly outside that entrance. Then follow a route to your chosen shops in a circle, so that you end up back at the spot that's closest to your car.

How to City Shop

When city shopping, a Social Diva can apply a lot of the same principles that work for mall shopping. We think a friend of Peg's put it best when she said, "Living in New York City is like having a mall in your back yard." And in a city, planning out your route is vital as well, because you'll be *carrying* your purchases from store to store. In order not to kill your arms, shoulders, and back, again we suggest making a game plan. Plot out what you want and where you need to go to get it. Try to restrict all your shopping to one area, if possible. If you must go out of your way for those Christian Louboutin platforms you can't live without, make it your first stop or your last shopping stop. This allows you to maximize your time in your concentrated area. Also, make small purchases first so that you're not carrying heavy or bulky items for longer than you absolutely must. This means you'd visit La Perla or Agent Provocateur (which are, by the way, our two top resources for very sexy and very Diva underthings) before IKEA. Once you're weighed down with domestic purchases, you can easily take a taxi home.

To Deliver or Carry?

Our rule of thumb: If the delivery costs less than the price of a taxi (or the items are just too big for you to manage), go ahead and have it delivered. It will save you a trip to the chiropractor in the long run, which saves you some money that could be used for a much-needed martini at day's end, or that beautiful beaded purse you couldn't decide if you wanted in black or green (now you can buy both!).

LIGHTS!

The lighting in changing rooms is almost always horrible, so put on your sunglasses. Yup, if you throw on your shades, you'll get a better idea of what you'll look like under more subdued light, since, unless it's office attire, you'll probably be wearing the outfit in the evening anyway!

How to Shop the Boutiques

What Diva doesn't love to walk up and down her favorite stretch of fashionable little shops? When it comes to boutique shopping, the ambience is definitely a whole lot more pleasant than the local mall. Nonetheless, a few key items must be addressed in order to have a successful boutique shopping trip.

IT'S ALL ABOUT ANGLES

 Try to choose boutiques that offer three-way mirrors in their changing rooms. You want to make sure your tush is fabulous in those new True Religions so that you know you look Diva-licious both coming and going!

Choose a shopping partner

Never go boutique shopping alone! You just won't feel comfortable parting with all that cash if you don't have someone to give you a second opinion on how you look. When choosing a boutique buddy, pick a friend who possesses the honesty and courage to tell you that you look awful but is also capable of honesty gently enough that you won't slip into a deep depression. Also, you want someone with you who likes to shop but doesn't like to spend too much herself: this will keep you from throwing away precious money on an item that you don't really need. Your perfect shopping companion also should excel in "per wear" mathematics, so that she can tell you: "If you pay $394 for these boots, and you wear them ten times, you're only paying $39.40 per outing." Brilliant!

Help at hand?

Sometimes you'll get the nicest sales assistant on Planet Earth, and sometimes you'll be treated like Julia Roberts when she shopped on Rodeo Drive for the first time in *Pretty Woman*. Either way, don't let the sales staff at a boutique affect you too much.

The majority of boutique salespeople work on commission, so if they seem to think you look *fabulous* in everything you try on (especially that $1,579 sweater), there's a good chance they're just trying to make the sale. (Can't blame them—we'd do the same thing!) Bottom line: rely on your and your shopping partner's judgment, not the sales assistant's.

If you're completely ignored, or the assistants give off some trendier-than-thou vibe, don't get nasty, just leave. They don't deserve your business anyway. Just remember to tell all your friends (especially the ones in high places, such as those who blog for SocialDiva.com) about your experience at that particular shop. A Diva can use her influence for good or evil, so bitchy boutique girls beware!

How to Sample Sale

Boutiques often hold sample sales of their designers' work. This is a great opportunity to get designer duds at a fraction of the regular price. The only problem? Typically, all the clothing is thrown into bins and in no particular order. An extra-large sweater could very well be in the same bin as an extra–small bikini top. We've known girls who have gone to a sample sale for six hours and come home with nothing. That's why you have to know how to shop the bins, and shop them smart!

THREE SIMPLE RULES FOR SAMPLE SALE-ING
1. Don't look for trendy items. Sample sales are better for basics and fabulous everyday items. Designer clothes are priced higher because they are meant to last a lifetime, not just until next season. When digging through the bins, keep your eye out for colors that you know are flattering on you, and fabrics that are of high quality. This will eliminate the need for you to examine at least forty percent of the items in each bin.

2. Have no shame. If you find something that you may want to buy, hang on to it. Don't put it back in the bin thinking you can come back and find it later...as it will most definitely be gone later. Of course, if you spot an indecisive shopper committing this sample-sale sin, and you just happen to love the item she foolishly put back, *grab it!* Her loss is your gain, and all's fair in sample sale-ing!

3. Know your size. Typically, sample sales are so huge that they have no space for changing rooms. That means you are flying blind unless you know your true size. If you're unsure of the fit, use a tape measure. There is nothing wrong with measuring your own inseam and comparing it to that gorgeous pair of houndstooth trousers.

SCIENCE AT WORK FOR YOU

Laws of proportion tell us that the neck is half the size of the waist, so when you're shopping for pants, jeans, or skirts in a hurry, and there is simply no time to try them on, fasten the waistband and then wrap it around your neck, making the two ends touch at the nape. If you have a little bit of slack left, there is a 99 percent chance the garment will fit you!

Some labels have invitation-only sample sales, so it helps to befriend someone in fashion PR, or alternatively get yourself on the relevant mailing lists. One Diva confidante got a Phillip Lim jacket reduced from $287 to $57 at an invite-only sale—hellooooo bargain!

How to Shop Vintage

When certain trends resurface, hitting your local vintage shops is a viable and affordable alternative to purchasing the vintage reproductions at Bloomie's or Saks. But remember, Diva, vintage stores can be tricky to navigate, so make sure you have lots of time available before you go hitting the stacks.

What's worth it (and what's not)

So you find this killer pair of vintage Levi's circa 1974, but they are a little too long and there appears to be a mustard stain on the pocket. Do you shell out the $49 for this piece of fashion history? We say, "Yes!" Hemming a pair of jeans only costs around $15 (if you can't do it yourself), and as for the stain, you would take your vintage purchase to the dry cleaner anyway because you *do* want to give them a good, *deep* cleaning before you wear them, right, Diva?

When it comes to buying vintage, don't be a perfectionist. The chances of finding a garment in mint condition are very, very slim, so when deciding whether to buy or not, consider the ease of the fix. If you need some help, follow this handy chart on pages 90-91 , which will tell you whether to snatch it or ditch it when it comes to buying vintage.

Is It Good Vintage?

THE PROBLEM	THE FIX	THE COST
Too long (leg/sleeve)	Hemming	About $15
Too big (chest/waist/hips)	Alteration	About $40
Small, inconspicuous stain	Professional cleaning	About $10
Big obvious stain	Professional cleaning	$10+
Too short	Alteration	About $30 + fabric costs
Too small (waist)	Alteration	About $30 + fabric costs
Too small (chest /hips)	Alteration	About $30 + fabric costs

SNATCH IT!	DITCH IT!
The easiest and cheapest alteration there is, so this is a must-buy.	
Pricier than hemming, but still an easy job for your local seamstress.	
No guarantee the stain will come out, but if not, you can camouflage it with an accessory.	
	No guarantees the stain will come out, and if it doesn't, the item was a waste of money.
	Chances of finding fabric that match exactly are slim, so ditch this one.
Typically, you cover your waist with a belt or top, so even if the fabric is not an exact match, you can still get away with it.	
	A difficult fix, and the chances of getting a good end result are not high. Assume the fashion gods are telling you it just wasn't meant to be.

How to Shop the Web

Shopping online is not only a huge time-saver, but also a way to avoid crowds of fellow shoppers. (Oh, and it's a really fun way to waste time at work, too—not that you ever would, right, Diva?) But to be a Diva-licious web-shopping warrior (and avoid massive delivery and return charges) there are a few things you have to know.

For shirts, tops, exercise wear, shoes, or other items that are simple to size, web browsing is a viable alternative to window-shopping. However, when hunting for pants, jeans, evening gowns, or any other item that is difficult to size, only surf stores that you have already shopped at online or in person. Sizing varies by brand, so just because you're a size 4 in Rock & Republic jeans doesn't mean that you will take that size in a pair of jeans by a different manufacturer. Bottom line: if you can look in your closet and find two similar items that fit you and are tagged with different sizes, you shouldn't be purchasing that item via the web.

We absolutely advise against buying lingerie online. Women have a hard enough time purchasing the correct bra size when they can actually try the bra on, never mind having to guesstimate what the size might be in a line they've never worn before. In addition, most lingerie is not returnable, so unless you're buying a replacement in the same style and size, you're going to be stuck with a $98 bra that your puppy can now use as a chew toy. Other items to avoid include expensive jewelry (because you won't be able to examine and hold the piece on a computer screen) and designer bags (because it's difficult to spot a fake when you can't see the bag up close).

HOW DO YOU MEASURE UP?

When purchasing clothing online, find websites that list the exact measurements of each garment. Compare those measurements to your own vital statistics to ensure a proper fit. If even these precautions fail, remember that some websites offer free delivery and free returns, which means if it doesn't fit your mistake has cost you nothing. Always keep an eye out for the details, Diva!

For a Social Diva, shopping is not just an activity, it's an Olympic event. There are rules to follow, strategies to consider, and you have to practice, practice, practice if you want to win the Gold. With our tips of the shopaholic's trade, you'll be on your way to a Diva-fied wardrobe in no time (and with as little drama as humanly possible).

TOP TEN MUST-HAVES FOR A DIVA-FIED SHOPPING TRIP
Here is what you should pack in your Birkin as you embark on a day of shopping bliss:

1. A list of what you need. This list will save you time and money because it will streamline your shopping efforts.

2. A list of what you want. This lists things you would like to have but don't require at this very moment. It's good to keep this list on you at all times, just in case you come across a huge sale.

3. Sunglasses. For adjusting lighting problems in changing rooms.

4. Tape measure. To see if something will fit without even trying it on.

5. Pair of Peds or thin socks. For trying on shoes.

6. Hand sanitizer. To use when that evil woman in the fragrance department gets spritz happy and attacks you with some awful scent. Rubbing the hand sanitizer on the affected areas will minimize the potency.

7. Thong. Necessary only if you aren't already wearing a thong. You'll want to slip one on to eliminate any underwear lines that might distract you from the overall fit of a garment.

8. Comfortable shoes. As if you didn't know, Diva, shopping involves an abundance of walking, and we don't want you breaking an ankle in four-inch stilettos!

9. Camera phone. If you're shopping alone and are unsure whether to purchase an item, send your shopping buddy a picture of it. There's no shame in asking for a second opinion, Diva!

10. This book. You might need to reference important Social Diva tips.

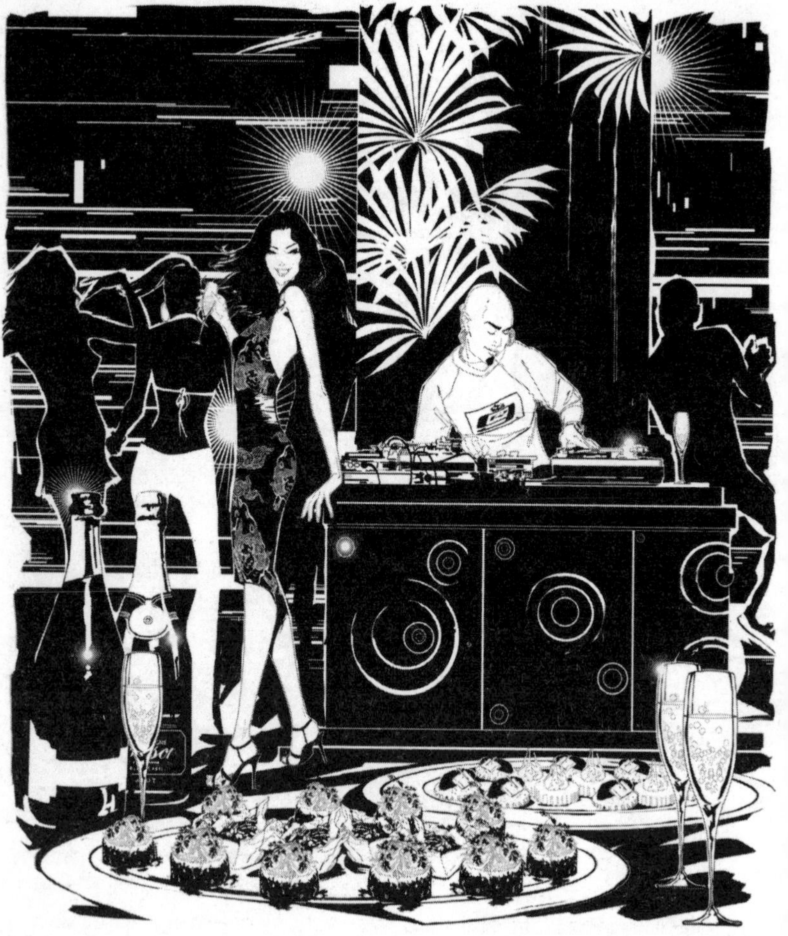

Chapter Six

DIVAS DON'T DO PLASTIC CUPS

How a Social Diva Does a House Party

House party: two words that can't help but remind you of the "good old days." The days of student apartments and Ramen noodles. The days of jumping into fountains with all your clothes on. The days when cheap alcohol was the cocktail de jour.

Everyone has good and bad memories of house parties, and Lexi's most vivid memory of one (based on what her friends told her the morning after) occurred at the tender age of twenty-one.

Our story begins with Lexi, in the kitchen of said house, doing what Lexi does best...outdrinking her male counterparts (an activity that she continues to participate in regularly to this very day, by the way). Everything was under control until two freshmen girls decided that it would be super fun to get some cherry ice pops from the freezer and dunk them into their tequila-filled plastic cups. (Lexi is still unsure as to why they were doing that, but she suspects that the blender might have been broken, and that dunking the frozen treats in alcohol was the next best thing to a margarita.)

Everything was hunky-dory until one of the girls started splatter-painting with her tequila-saturated ice pop leaving vivid red stains all over the kitchen and everyone in it. This little faux pas resulted in two massive stains on Lexi's brand-new, very expensive silk top, and one freshman girl with a bloody nose.

That being said, you can see why we decided that, fun as it was to play underage drinking games and engage in fisticuffs with schoolmates, we'll be damned if we ever go to a house party like that ever again.

Nonetheless, the house party lives on, and still shows up in the calendar of all Social Divas. Though nowadays things are done a little differently. We go to house parties where we leave with a goodie bag containing items bearing the Chanel logo, rather than leave with some cheerleader's regurgitated dinner on our shoes.

Not sure what constitutes a house party? Well, it could be a girls' night out hosted by your best gal pal, or an Oscar party thrown by a colleague, or a neighbor's barbeque to celebrate the Super Bowl. All these get-togethers count as house parties.

And since you're at an age where Doritos are no longer a suitable party contribution, we've compiled the following pages to guide you through preparations for attending a house party.

House Party Haute Couture

First things first, Divas! And first things are outfit decisions.

Sometimes you can let the invitation be your guide. For example, if an invite calls for black tie, you should probably wear something long and dressy. Unfortunately, most house party invitations don't specify attire, so it's up to you to work it out on your own. The best way to do this is to take a quick assessment of two very important house party variables: Occasion and Orientation.

Occasion refers, of course, to the reason for partying. Dressing for an occasion is usually pretty simple. For example, you're not going to wear a wool sweater to your brother's pool party in July, or a tube top to your five-year-old niece's birthday party in November, right? Right!

Themed house parties fall under the occasion variable as well. In this case the invitation will request specific attire—for example, Dress Like Your Favorite Charlie's Angel, or Wear Your Favorite Green Hat.

If all else fails and you're still unsure, call the hostess and ask what she will be wearing for her party (because it's virtually impossible to be dubbed "inappropriately dressed" if you're sporting the same style as the party host).

> ## DRESS UP!
>
> If you've been invited to a themed house party and the invitation calls for you to wear a costume or dress as a character, do not call your hostess and ask if people are "really dressing up." She is expecting everyone to arrive in costume, or else she wouldn't have put it on the invitation. Oh, and never, ever disregard the invite and show up in ordinary clothes. Social Divas are not party poopers.

Orientation refers to the type of people on the guest list, and dressing to suit the party's orientation can be tricky when there are lots of different types attending and each has a different idea of what it's OK to wear. Think about it this way: people who work at investment firms typically wear suits every day, whereas those who work in advertising tend to dress much more casually. If both types meet at the same party, the chances are they'll be dressed very differently from each other.

There are three main categories of orientation—family, friend, and company—and every house party you attend can be classified as one of these. Here are a few tips for dressing around all three.

Family-oriented parties

If the majority of guests at a house party are your own family, you can be pretty relaxed because you don't really have to impress anyone. After all, just about everyone present remembers seeing you in braces and Z. Cavariccis when you were twelve, so you'd have to be wearing a burlap sack with a yeti strapped to your back to look worse than that.

Speaking of the rare times when you've looked mildly unfabulous (and we've all had them), on certain occasions at family-oriented house parties it might behoove you to dress badly (gasp!). Here's a little trick to try if you "accidentally" spent your car payment on a new pair of hunter green Miss Sixty boots: show up at a family house party looking as if you slept on the street the night before (i.e., hair in disarray, smudgy makeup, dirty jeans…). Chances are you might just score a check for a considerable amount from your Aunt Rita, after she informs you that you *obviously* need some new clothes…and a decent haircut.

Attention, Divas! Under no circumstances should you follow the above guidelines if you are attending a house party thrown by someone else's family. What would your mother think if your boyfriend showed up wearing a sheer top with a lacy bra and red lipstick? Well, all right, first she would think he was gay, and *then* she would think he was being totally inappropriate. When attending a house party thrown by a family other than your own, you want to look classy yet casual. We're not talking about wearing your mother's pearls here, we're merely suggesting that for this particular occasion perhaps you should leave the push-up bra at home.

RELATIVELY WASTEFUL

 Don't waste a cute outfit on your own relatives. Save it for an occasion when it could reap dividends in terms of male interest.

Friend-oriented parties

If you are a friend of the host or hostess, just wear what you usually wear to house parties. These people are your closest pals, and they already love you and your Social Diva style. In this case, throw the word *appropriate* out the window and just do what you do (and wear what you wear) best.

If you are just a "friend of a friend" at the party, consult the person who invited you along to find out what kind of crowd will be there, and where to draw the line on cleavage exposure.

If you're crashing a house party, we suggest wrapping a bed sheet around you as a toga and putting a lampshade on your head. Just kidding—as if a Social Diva would ever have to crash a party!

Company-oriented parties

Don't stray too much from what you would normally wear to work. The last thing you need is for your boss to create some elaborate reason to fire you, when the actual cause of her ill will is that her husband was staring at your Daisy Duke shorts for a good chunk of the evening.

If you have a job that requires you to be a nine-to-five slave to the suit, keep your office party outfit pretty sober, too. Some boot-cut khaki pants and a form-fitting polo shirt keep the cuteness factor, but still work well for the company picnic. But don't forget to throw a dash of "fabulous" into your frock at these events: carry a killer bag or drape a designer scarf around your neck.

If you work in a casual setting, wear whatever you normally wear to work, but spice it up a bit. For example, if you usually wear solid colors to the office, don a fabulous print for the party. Or if you're typically in sneakers during the work day, throw on some leopard platform stilettos to go with your party get-up.

Bottom line, Diva: wear what makes you feel good. Even if you have to "tone down" your style in order to be dressed appropriately for a particular occasion, always incorporate something that is totally and undeniably you. If nothing else, it will make you feel more comfortable with your ensemble. For example, Lexi almost always wears black toenail polish. (Yes, we mentioned earlier that your toes should always match your tips when it comes to nail polish, but in this particular case, mismatching your digits so that you can keep your job, is A-OK with us!) That way, whether she's in the boardroom making a presentation about fourth-quarter sales projections or dancing wildly at a Rolling Stones concert, she always has a splash of her own personal glam-rock style on her.

PARTY ESSENTIALS
No Social Diva should walk out the door without her bag of party tricks! Before you leave your pad to head to any given shindig, stock your Louis Vuitton with the following items:

Breath mints: Because you never know how much garlic your hostess is going to use, and you never, ever know where your lips might end up later.

Brown eye pencil: This multi-functional wonder can be used to turn under-eye mascara smudge into a "smoky eye look," transform an unexpected zit into a dazzling beauty mark, and can even be employed as a makeshift writing instrument.

Ibuprofen and Alka-Seltzer: To give hangovers a swift kick in the pants before they can begin their reign of terror.

iPod: Because, as a Social Diva, you will inevitably be called upon to save the day if the hostess runs out of decent party tunes.

Neutral scarf: Can be used to cover an unexpected love bite, or employed as a hair wrap or ponytail holder to mask a hair meltdown should the weather turn sour.

Oversized sunglasses: If you're a Social Diva, you have no curfew, so there's always the distinct possibility that you'll arrive back at your digs after the sun has already risen. In this case, you'll need these babies to protect your peepers from post-drinking retina burns.

What Else to Take

A Social Diva never shows up to a house party empty-handed: cheap is not our style. Unless you're going to a ladies' night poker game, strolling into a house party with a bag of pretzels and a six-pack of beer is wrong.

Enter the hostess gift. This little token is not just a polite gesture, it's pretty much a requirement for house-party entry in Social Diva circles. A hostess gift should be something small but utterly fabulous. Here are some of our favorite gifts to give our most Diva-licious hostesses.

HOSTESS GIFTS

For the hostess with a sweet tooth...
Designer chocolates made by Godiva.

For the hostess with a standing spa appointment...
Aromatherapy candles made by Archipelago.

For the hostess with a stressful day job...
Luxury bath soaps made by Lush or L'Occitane.

For the hostess with the best manners you've ever encountered...
Timeless stationery made by Kate Spade or Crane & Co.

For the hostess with a ridiculously busy schedule...
Fashionable notebook or a personal organizer made by Smythson.

For the hostess with an accessory addiction...
Lacquer jewelry box from Anthropologie.

For the hostess with the mostest...
Her very own copy of *How to Be a Social Diva!*

In lieu of a hostess gift, house-party guests typically make an offering of alcohol or something delicious to nibble. Social Divas are most certainly *not* typical house-party-goers, and with our busy schedules we sometimes just don't have time to go out and find the perfect hostess gift. So if really pressed to go the food or drink route, the least you can do is do it Diva-style. Pick up a fabulous sushi platter for your hostess's buffet table, or shell out a bit extra to get her a really nice bottle of wine or champagne.

BRING YOUR OWN

 If the invitation to the house party states BYOB (bring your own bottle), you are officially exempt from presenting a hostess gift.

The Party Mingle

A Social Diva must be an expert in the art of mingling. It's not a skill you're born with; rather, it's something you practice for years to hone it down to a fine art. Here are some helpful rules to set you on your way.

FIVE RULES OF HOUSE-PARTY MINGLING
1. Look happy. Smile…a lot. Nobody wants to party with a moping, though very well-dressed, wallflower.

2. Shake hands "like a man." Most people, especially those of the male persuasion, are taken aback when they shake hands with a woman who has a firm grip. The sheer element of surprise will make you even more memorable than you already are. Additionally, shaking hands "like a man" implies to the person you're meeting that you are a strong, independent, self-sufficient woman…in other words, a Social Diva!

3. Pete and re-Pete. When you meet someone new, repeat his or her name in your head at least three times, or mentally associate the person's name with something familiar to you. For example, let's say you are introduced to someone named Troy. In your mind think about the movie *Troy*, which starred the hunk-a-licious Brad Pitt. Now, it's not very likely that you'll forget about Brad Pitt, right, Diva? With these two methods under your belt, you will certainly be more likely to recall a new friend's name, even after you've had a few cocktails.

4. Dodge artfully. To escape gracefully from an unwanted flirtatious advance at a house party, utter the following: "Hold that thought. I have to go check on my kids. It will only take a sec—they're just outside in the car."

Peg prefers the "high-maintenance hide-out technique," in which she will excuse herself to the ladies' room and spend about thirty minutes primping. Given that men have such a short attention span, chances are they'll be bugging someone else by the time she resurfaces. If that doesn't work, she'll grab her trusty iPhone and announce that she has a missed a call from so-and-so about an upcoming appearance or VIP ticket, and insist that she must return the call. Then she'll conveniently disappear so that she can mix and mingle with others, safely away from Mr. Wrong.

5. Guard your number. If you are totally disinterested in a man who asks for your phone number, smile sweetly and give it to him…with one incorrect digit. *He* gets an ego-boost and you avoid an outrageous number of unwanted voice mails.

Everybody wins! We know what you're thinking, "But Diva, why change only one digit?" Good question! Let's pretend that the cosmos aligned, Mercury went into retrograde, cows jumped over the moon, and somehow he ends up with your *real* phone number. If he confronts you about the number you originally gave him, you can just say that you were little soused when you wrote it down, and must have "accidentally" written it wrong.

Making an Exit

When the champagne is spent, the sushi has disappeared, and the hostess's brother tries to strike up a conversation by muttering something that begins with "You know what makes me sad…" a Diva knows it's time to take her final bows and move on to her next adventure. Here are some effective methods and exceptional lines to help you make a memorable (and time-efficient) exit.

The Faux Exec Exit: "What time is it? Three a.m. already! I must be off; I have a meeting with Kimora Lee Simmons's people in six hours!"

The Stealth Operation Exit: Slip quietly out the door without being noticed. That way, when everyone realizes you've gone, you'll be the talk of the room—and Lord knows you'll love knowing you have that attention!

The SJP Exit: As Sarah Jessica Parker might well say, "I have to go, my shoes have an early curfew."

The Jet-Setter Exit: "I have to get home so I can pack for my trip to the French Riviera."

The Courtney Love Exit: "I'm starting a new detox regime in an hour."

The Mysterious Exit: "I have to go…I have another *thing*."

The Bond Exit: This is the Social Diva's personal favorite. Hide in the ladies' room and call your hostess from your cell (make sure you dial *67 before calling so that you can't be identified through caller ID). When she answers, disguise your voice and say, "Would you be so kind as to tell [insert your name] that her driver is waiting outside?"

The Day After

Call the hostess and thank her for the party. It's common courtesy, and it's a great opportunity to gossip about the previous evening's events (as if you missed anything!). Or, if you are a busy Social Diva already preparing for your next event, simply drop her a quick thank-you note via snail mail or e-mail. Since you have great manners, we know you have a stack of thank-you cards in your desk drawer just ready to go.

At first glance, a house party may seem like something from the past that should stay in the past, but in the schedule of a Social Diva house parties are still alive and well, and can be highly satisfactory when you do them right (which we *know* you will, Diva).

Chapter Seven

PARTY HARD, BUT DO IT FOR A CAUSE

How a Social Diva Does a Fundraiser or Benefit

Social Divas love to be part of...well, everything! That's why we encourage all Divas to get involved with local and national organizations, and give a little bit of Diva love back to the community.

Benefits, fundraisers, and charity auctions are excellent ways for a Social Diva do-gooder to use her influence and popularity among the masses to help out a good cause. And at the same she'll gain yet another opportunity to get dressed up and mingle with the beautiful people.

If you're a charitable Diva (and we're sure you are), you probably attend a lot of these shindigs already. But if you're a fundraising novice, or unsure of the protocol for these high-class soirées, read on for a step-by-step Diva guide to maneuvering your way through a charitable function.

Dress It Up, Up, and Up

When choosing an ensemble for an upcoming fundraiser or benefit, let the invitation be your guide.

Most national organizations throw black-tie affairs, and that means it's time to give your vintage Halston gown an airing, ice yourself down with diamonds, and dig up your satin clutch bag, Diva. A function that requires black tie is nothing to fool with. Although fundraisers and benefits are meant to be enjoyable, they have a serious undertone, making a dress code more stringent than what you might be used to. For example, if you strut into the ballroom at your friend's black-tie wedding decked out in a magnificent, knee-length cocktail dress, the hosts won't think any less of you (in fact, they'll probably commend you on your daring yet tactful wardrobe choice). But if you were to wear the same ensemble to a black-tie benefit, you will look tremendously out of place in the sea of dinner jackets and ball gowns.

At less formal charitable functions we suggest dressing just a touch above the required dress code. For example, if the invitation calls for casual attire, deck yourself out in your hippest evening pantsuit (you know, the silky winter-white one that is just a little too cheeky to wear to work but still stunningly refined) and complement it with some fantastically embellished strappy sandals from Jimmy Choo.

If the invitation leaves you unsure about the proper attire, try to imagine the wardrobe of a classic Hollywood starlet (think 1940s or 1950s), and emulate that style icon for the night.

For example, whenever Lexi is dressing for a charitable function, she asks herself this question: "What would Sophia Loren wear?" (Sophia Loren being Lexi's absolute favorite Diva of all time). La Loren's style is the very definition of classic elegance with a touch of sexy sophistication. As Lexi has observed, "You know that very thin line between not enough cleavage and too much cleavage? Sophia Loren invented that."

LOUNGE SUIT DRESS CODE

When you come across an invitation that calls for a "lounge suit," the host is asking the gentlemen to wear suits (with or without a tie these days) and women to wear dressy trousers or a frock. It certainly doesn't mean wearing what you would "lounge" around the house in (i.e., your pajamas)!

Working the Room

Diva, please note that it is best to treat a fundraiser or benefit as an elegant business function: this translates to "dress like you mean it" and "be on your best behavior." For a Social Diva, that means you want to work the room—actually, more like *own* the room—but do it in a manner a little less boisterous than your usual Diva style. For example, let's say that at an Annual Breast Cancer Awareness Gala the DJ starts playing "Dancing Queen," which happens to be your favorite song of all time. Although it may be appropriate to stand on a chair and explode into your best ABBA impersonation at your cousin's wedding, it is *not* OK at a charitable function. We know you'll see the distinction here, Diva.

EAT A CRACKER, DIVA!

Never go to a fundraiser or benefit feeling hungry. If you attack the canapés with too much vigor, you risk being remembered as the girl who hogged all the vol-au-vents.

Well, now that we've identified the *wrong* way to work (or own) the room at a charity event, it's time to discuss the Social Diva way.

HOW TO WORK THE ROOM

Tip 1. Memorize in advance the names of key players in the organization. These should be listed on the organization's website. This will lower the chances of forgetting the name of a VIP you really want to meet if you "accidentally" sip too much champagne.

Tip 2. Handshakes are the typical greeting at these events, so if you're carrying anything around with you (i.e., your satin clutch or your glass of wine) always hold it in your left hand. This eliminates the need to fumble around with your things before you can extend your right hand to meet a new and possibly interesting acquaintance.

Tip 3. Always introduce yourself to everyone at your table *before* you sit down. Not only does this make you appear genuine and gracious (as if they didn't know that already), but it also allows you to avoid those awkward mid-conversation introductions that might occur after you've been chatting with someone for a while.

HOW TO DO THE DOUBLE KISS

In Europe the double-kiss greeting (left cheek first, Diva) is pretty standard once you're on more than nodding terms. If you find yourself in a situation where kissing has superseded handshaking, you can carry whatever your little Diva heart desires because you don't need an empty hand in order to greet people properly.

DIVAS DON'T DO DRIBBLES

If canapés are served at a function, stay away from those that are potentially drippy or cannot be eaten in one bite. You don't want to be remembered as the guest who had a dribble of mayonnaise on her chin.

Networking the Room

There will be many, *many* important individuals sharing the room with you, Diva, and fundraisers and benefits are seriously great opportunities not only to support a worthy cause but also to expand your ever-growing list of contacts. However, your number-one reason for attendance is to cheer on the organization, not yourself. If you forget this golden rule, networking during a charitable function can come off as rude and inappropriate. Here are a few tips on how to do it the right way.

TIPS FOR NETWORKING THE ROOM

Tip 1. Do your homework! Know your facts about the organization and the cause it supports. If you meet one of the head honchos but are unable to converse about the very reason for your attendance, it not only looks shallow but virtually eliminates any possibility of befriending that person on a personal or business level.

Tip 2. Find out about what the key players bring to the charitable table. This will give you plenty of conversational ammunition when you are introduced to them, and the longer the exchange continues, the better the chance of arranging a tête-à-tête to discuss working on a project together.

Tip 3. Take your business cards, but know when to bring them out. If someone asks you for a card, it is absolutely OK to hand one over. But if it's up to you to initiate the business card exchange, always rationalize it by relating it to the conversation. For example, if you are discussing future events for the organization, you can say, "Oh, really? I would love to be involved in promoting the event, if you could use my help. May I give you my card so that we can touch base about this sometime soon?"

THE BUSINESS CARD SWAP

 When giving out business cards at a high-class function, never, ever say something as generic and casual as, "Here's my card...call me." Always rationalize the exchange and ask the potential recipient, "May I give you my card?" It's just common courtesy, Diva!

So now that you've been schooled in fundraiser fashion and are more familiar with the protocol for benefit behavior, all you have left to do, Diva, is find out which charitable organizations represent the issues that are most important to you.

LOOK IT UP

Remember to do your research on any organization you want to be involved with. After all, you don't want your donations to end up in the wrong hands.

Being Charitable on a Budget

We sympathize with the fact that a lot of Divas are on a tight budget, and that writing a massive check to your favorite cause is sometimes just not an option. But as a Social Diva, you know that it's important to support good causes, and even if you never attend a high-roller fundraiser or benefit in your lifetime, you want to get involved anyway. And that's a great attitude. We *love* it!

There are soooo many things you can do to help out less fortunate Divas! Here's a list of five easy things you can do to make your community a little more Diva-fied—and it won't cost you a penny!

1. Donate your old cell phone. Lots of charities would love to receive your old mobile phones. They raise funds by selling them to "green" companies who repair and/or reformat them, and the phones are passed on to people in countries around the world who cannot afford a cell phone. That's what we call safety in numbers, Diva!

2. Donate your old ball gown or bridesmaid dress. Many impoverished teenage girls will not attend their proms because they have nothing to wear. We simply *cannot* let this injustice continue, Divas! Donate your elegant throw-aways so that these girls get the dress of their dreams for next to nothing (anyway, it's not like you're going to wear it again).

3. Hold your own canned food drive. Collect all those cans of baked beans and soup that have been collecting dust in your pantry, and encourage all your Diva pals to stop by your apartment with their canned food. Pack them all in a box and drop it off at your local homeless shelter. We can almost guarantee that what you and your fellow Divas scrounge up will be enough to feed at least one family for a whole week.

4. Mentor a student. It's safe to say that Social Divas are some of the best role models for young ones. We're self-sufficient, intelligent, witty, and utterly fabulous! Contact local schools and children's organizations to find out how you can take a

Baby Diva under your wing, and teach her all the little things she needs to know about Diva-dom!

5. Volunteer your time at a center for victims of domestic violence. A few seconds on Google, and you can find your nearest refuge that caters to women and children who have been victims of domestic violence. Social Divas are perfect for this kind of work because we are all about Girl Power (and we apologize profusely for the Spice Girls reference). At centers such as these, you can help victims by listening to their stories and offering support to rebuild their confidence and self-image. Divas don't get pushed around!

DONATING PAYS

 Don't forget, Diva, that anything—goods or money—that you donate to a charitable organization, including entrance fees to charitable events, is tax deductible. How very "help me— help you"!

Divas Do Awareness

Most of us know that October is Breast Cancer Awareness Month, and December is AIDS Awareness Month, but what about the other ten months of the year? Yes, we wondered too, so here is a list of awareness events devoted to serious issues that affect women all around the globe, along with months dedicated to slightly more minor debacles. Google any of the following topics to find out how you can help support the cause!

A SOCIAL DIVA'S CHARITABLE EVENTS CALENDAR

JANUARY
World Leprosy Week
You may think that leprosy is a dead issue, but it is still a problem in developing countries, and it needs our attention, Diva. And since you, as a Diva, have such a reputation for being in the know, the best thing you can do to help is to start telling people the facts about leprosy, that it still exists, and that it continues to destroy lives. The more people who know, the better chance there is of wiping it out for good.

FEBRUARY
International Childhood Cancer Day
Cancer affects millions of little Divas every day, all over the world. Find out what you can do to help children with cancer get the best treatment and care, regardless of their parents' financial situation. Just like adult Divas, baby Divas deserve only the best!

MARCH
International Women's Day
This is the day to celebrate how utterly fantastic women truly are, as if you don't celebrate that every single day, Diva!

Self-Injury Awareness Day
Utilize your Diva mingling skills to raise awareness about self-injury, and use your knack for being able to talk about the taboo to help individuals who suffer from this behavioral issue.

APRIL
Africa Malaria Day

Malaria kills 1.1 million people every year, most of them children. Even worse, malaria is a totally preventable and treatable disease. Use this day to find out what you can do to help our fellow Divas in Africa fight to control this epidemic.

MAY
World Asthma Day

Many Divas have asthma, or know someone who does. In fact, we know someone who had an asthma attack when she saw her Visa card statement after a shopping extravaganza at Prada. Use this day to find out how you can help improve asthma treatments worldwide so that your Diva pals can keep their breathing under control when bills arrive!

JUNE
World Blood Donor Day

This is a day for blood services to thank their donors for providing support for patients across the entire globe. Help celebrate by going out and giving some blood yourself. After all, everyone could use a little extra Diva DNA, right?

Osteoporosis Awareness Month

Also known as fragile bone disease, osteoporosis affects four times as many women as men—a good reason to drink your milk, Diva! If not prevented, or if left untreated, it can progress silently until bones break and crumble.

JULY
World Population Awareness Day
The World Population Awareness Day was inaugurated in 1988 by the United Nations Population Fund to mark July 11, 1987, when the world's population hit 5 billion. Spend the day trying to get to know as many fabulous folks as possible—you could make a lot of new networking contacts, get the lowdown on a shoe discount, and meet a new Diva-licious friend all in the same day. After all, mingling is one of the things Divas do best!

AUGUST
World Breastfeeding Week
This event is bigger than you think, Diva: it is recognized in over 120 countries. Use this week to find out what breastfeeding really brings to a Baby Diva's life.

SEPTEMBER
World Alzheimer's Day
Think about how horrible you feel when you forget a friend's birthday. Imagine, then, how frustrating it would be to forget who that friend actually is. Find out what you can do to help individuals confronting dementia, and the families who care for them.

OCTOBER
Breast Cancer Awareness Month
Participate in a "Walk for the Cure," learn how to give yourself a breast examination, and discover how mammograms can help early detection. This is a *big* month for Divas because every three minutes another woman is diagnosed with breast cancer.

NOVEMBER
World Diabetes Day
Millions of people have diabetes and it has no cure. In November, diabetes organizations worldwide help the public to learn more about diabetes and the associated risks. Get involved, Diva, and help find the cure that will allow diabetes patients to enjoy the same Godiva chocolates you love so much!

DECEMBER
World AIDS Day
This is a day to celebrate the progress made in the battle against AIDS, along with bringing the remaining challenges of this disease into focus. See what you can do to help find a cure or to provide support for those who have contracted the disease—because, as great as you look in red, just wearing that ribbon is not enough.

So, Diva, whether it's a fundraiser, a benefit, or just a donation, you can do something to help make this world a little more Diva-licious! It's just as we always say: Social Divas should use their influence over the masses only for good...kind of like Superman...so does that make you a Super Diva? Umm, totally!

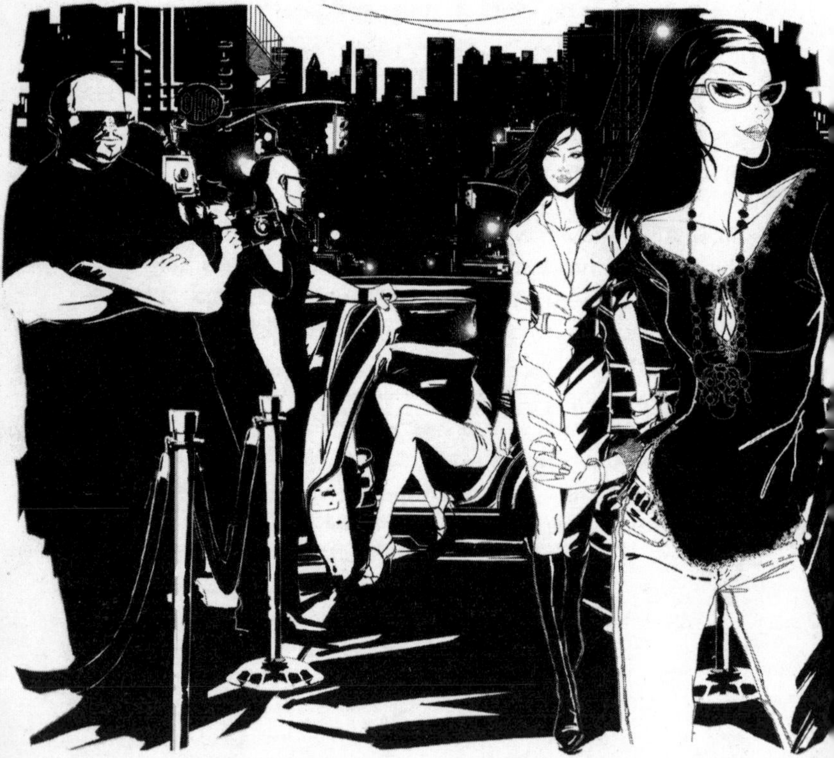

Chapter Eight

WE'VE ONLY SEEN VELVET ROPES IN OUR REARVIEW

How a Social Diva Does the Club Scene

Ah, yes, club-hopping…you'll never be too good for it. That is, you'll never be too good for it as long as you know where to hang out, who to party with, and how to score a complimentary bar tab. Divas know that club-hopping is just no fun if you're paying for every cocktail in a venue with no VIP room, surrounded by amateur club-goers. So, Diva, when it's Friday night and your schedule states that you've been cordially invited to the opening of the newest, hottest, most trendy club in town, we suggest you leave work a little early to get in your disco nap (see page 52) and still have time to prepare for the ab fab night that lies ahead of you. As you'll see in this chapter, there are lots of things to consider when it comes to hitting the clubs like a Diva.

Dress to Impress
(Not to Gross Us Out)

When dressing for a night out at the clubs, pick something light and breathable—after all, wild dancing in a seething crowd of people can make it very hot and steamy.

Now, by "light and breathable" we do not mean extra small and super-exposing. Divas always look sexy, but always leave something to the imagination. A little cleavage, a little leg, even a little midriff if your stomach is rockin', is totally fine, but anything more than a little is just plain too much. Divas, we implore you to refrain from donning hoochie-mama club gear (i.e., anything made out of polyester that could be described by onlookers as a "sling of fabric"). Bottom line, if you look like a million bucks, people will treat you like a million bucks. If you look like a hooker, people are going to treat you like a hooker. Let's keep it civilized here, Divas!

When clubbing, we prefer the half-and-half look—namely, half casual, half dressy—because it will work for just about any club, regardless of the dress code. For example, if you're wearing high-end denim below, give it some pizazz by adding a beaded halter top and some sexy stilettos. If you're wearing black trousers, balance your look with a men's white tank top and some fabulous jewelry like a statement necklace from Kenneth Jay Lane.

As for shoes, make your decision based on the kind of club-goer you are. For example, Lexi loves to hit the dance floor and show off the moves she picked up from Justin Timberlake videos, so she prefers to wear stacked heel shoes with a rounded toe. The stacked heels allow her better balance than a stiletto, and the rounded toe keeps her little tootsies from being pinched while strutting her stuff on the dance floor. Peg, on the other hand, is a mingler rather than a dancer (unless the DJ starts spinning New Wave, and then you have to physically remove her from atop the speakers when it's time to leave). More than likely, you'll see Peg bouncing from table to table greeting everyone she knows in the joint at least once (depending on their level of hotness). As she will probably be seated for most of the night, she can get away with anything from strappy stilettos to six-inch platform boots. Go, Diva!

How a Social Diva Fits Her Life Into a Clutch Bag

The clutch is the most do-able bag for the club scene. It's small, it's easy to hold while dancing or mingling, and it makes a superb Diva-licious statement! But if we've heard it once, we've heard it a million times: "How do you fit everything into such a small bag?" Easy, Diva! All you have to do is streamline. Here's what you can effectively pack into a clutch bag with room to spare.

Credit card: A smart Diva never leaves home without her plastic.

Four $20 Bills: Excessive small change is a no-no when carrying a clutch: it's heavy and it wastes precious space.

ID: You look soooo young, Diva, how else are you supposed to get a cocktail?

Key: This can be the key to your car or your apartment, depending on how you arrive at the venue (see the bag tips and Lexi's key trick in chapter 9). But be sure to remove it from your huge key ring, Diva…there's no room for the whole thing!

Lip gloss: Shiny lips are a must because they give you some color and make you sparkle.

Cell phone: For doorman drama (you'll see what we mean in a sec), candid photography, and finding your friends if you get lost in the crowd.

Tester vial of perfume: With this little item, you can refresh yourself and effectively block out the odor of the smelly crowds around you.

Travel-size pack of baby wipes: These will help you to clean up any cocktail mishaps, such as spilling your Cosmo on your True Religions, and protect you from icky germs in the ladies' room.

SAFETY FIRST, DIVA!

Whenever you go out for a night on the town, always stash an emergency twenty in your shoe or underwear. That way if something terrible happens (such as having your bag stolen), you'll always have enough cash to take a cab home. (Also, keeping $20 where it's difficult to get to will deter you from spending it on anything else.)

Getting Past the Gatekeeper

Social Divas are always on the door list. Always. But for your own sanity, call the individual who put you there before turning up at the door. It's just a ten-second phone call to make certain that adding your name plus a guest hasn't slipped your contact's mind in the midst of the pre-opening rush.

If, by some act of God, you arrive at the door and your name is *not* on the list, don't fret, and certainly don't go all feisty in a Diva-esque rampage against the doorman. The most important thing to remember in a situation like this is to remain calm: the more you fuss, the more the other people waiting will know that your name has magically disappeared from the list. Which is super-embarrassing. So, to avoid negative thoughts from swirling in the minds of the people behind you, follow these steps.

THREE STEPS TO AVOID DOORMAN DRAMA
1. Get that frazzled expression off your face! You must keep your composure and appear as if nothing is wrong. Plus, worry lines on your forehead can be a real bummer.

2. Extract your Blackberry from your clutch and dial the contact who was supposed to put you on the list.

3. Quietly move out of line with the phone to your ear. This will make it look as if you are calling a friend to meet you out front, as opposed to calling your contact to give him or her the news that your entry is a no-go.

If your club contact is a halfway decent human being, he or she will come to the door and rectify the situation. If you can't get hold of your contact, or he claims "There is nothing I can do," you have several options:

- Flash your faux press pass at the doorman and claim to be a reporter for a local gossip paper (always a guaranteed entry).

- Depending on the number of people at the door, a little restraint and tolerance can get you and your Diva pals past that rope. If you are next to the doorman, you can try to talk your way in by saying, "I'm not sure what happened. Tony Cool promised he'd put my name down." Be kind and empathetic to the chaos the door person has to work in, Diva, and you might just see that magic rope unhooked for you after all.

- Leave. If all else fails, we suggest bouncing your Diva-licious little bottom out of there. If this particular club doesn't have the kind of managers who know how to cater to very important patrons, you don't really want to be there anyway. Plus, Social Divas can make or break a new club, which means that if you're not going, nobody worth mentioning is going either, especially after you've spread the word.

Should the dreaded not-on-the-list situation ever arise, don't feel hurt. You're not an unlisted loser—you're a done-wrong Diva! It happens to more people than you think, and for the craziest reasons. For example, Lexi went to a book party at a new club in Atlanta recently and encountered this very same debacle. Told that her name was not on the list, she followed the aforementioned steps and finally chose to leave the venue (Step 3). However, she made sure to alert all her fashionista friends to the substandard treatment she received, advising them to spend their club-hopping nights anywhere but at Club X.

It later transpired that the promoter had given the doorman the wrong guest list on the night in question, resulting in an abundance of influential VIPs (including Lexi) being turned away at the door. So many influential VIPs, in fact, that the club closed its doors within a month of opening due to a lack of patrons. *That's* the power of a Social Diva!

PATIENCE IS A DIVINE VIRTUE

Be patient with the person at the door while he searches for your name. Sometimes event promoters neglect to put lists in alphabetical order, plus they may have multiple lists, and that makes the door person's life a living hell. Show a little compassion and wait patiently for him or her to find your moniker…it will pay off next time when the door guy remembers your face and allows you to jump the line.

VIP? Oh, That's Me!

On a typical club-going excursion, Social Divas will get past the door with ease (and without paying a cover), and once through, it's time to make your way to where the beautiful people are—the VIP room.

Social Divas on the door list are almost always on the VIP list. If by some chance, you were promised VIP status but another doorman flub gets in your way, it's time to work your feminine wiles, Divas! Here's a foolproof technique to shimmy your way into VIP treatment.

The VIP room shimmy

Slip the man at the velvet rope a twenty (but not your emergency twenty because getting into VIP does not qualify as an emergency), or offer to buy him a cocktail if he lets you and your gal pal through. Tell him that it's her birthday and her boyfriend just dumped her, and you really, *really* want her to have a good time tonight. With these tactics you appeal to his sympathetic side, his sexual side (the side of him that thinks he might have a chance with your friend, which, of course, he probably doesn't, but hey, who are we to trample on his dreams, right?), and if he's gay, he's pleased that he just made twenty bucks. No matter what kind of guy he is, with this story you are *so* in!

If the VIP room is reserved for a private party, your chances of getting in are lower than usual. In this situation, try to find out who makes up the party, and adjust your scheme to fit. For example, if it's a private event for a celeb, wait until a member of his or her entourage takes a break from the room, then strike up a conversation. Who knows, you guys might share a mutual love of *Sex and the City* reruns, resulting in a bona fide invitation back to VIP territory.

If you're not really into the VIP scene, a few other places can be found in just about every club where the hipster crowd hangs out.

A SOCIAL DIVA'S FAVORITE PLACES TO PERCH

Near the side of the bar: Club rats* and serious alcoholics are typically found holding down the fort at the front of the bar (and, in turn, making it very difficult for anyone else to get a cocktail—thanks a lot, guys!). But Divas hang out at the side of the bar. This is an area that always spawns some fun chitchat, allows you to get to know the hot bartender a little bit better, and you're just two steps away from a refill on your martini. Fab-u, baby!

*Club rat (n.) A person who is always at a club. No, really, always. Club rats sleep their days away right next to the velvet ropes just so they can be the first inside when the doors open. Divas steer clear!

On the sofa: There's always a sofa, and it's usually the best seat in the house. Find it and park your sassy little rear on it! Club owners put sofas in the best people-watching areas, and people-watching is, of course, one of a Social Diva's favorite pastimes.

By the back door: Hanging out here not only serves its purpose as a means of quick escape from an unexpected, full-frontal, ex-boyfriend attack, but it's also the preferred method of exit and entry for all celebrities and Very, Very VIP types, making it a great spot to get your mingle on.

Upstairs: Just like the sofa, there is almost always an upstairs, but a lot of club-goers don't know about it. You can use this spot as your own little Diva perch from which you can watch everything as it unfolds below you.

DO A LAP!

When scoping the club scene, always do a lap around the joint before committing to a location. You want to see everything that's going on before you settle into one spot. You wouldn't want to miss anything, right, Diva?

Divas Don't Do Tabs

Social Diva VIPs will typically have their bar tabs comped (treated as complimentary) by the house, but if that's not the case, scoring a free drink or two has never been a problem for any woman...especially a Diva. Here are some foolproof techniques that will help you keep your bar tab as small as possible.

A SOCIAL DIVA'S TOP FOUR TAB BUSTERS

The Big Spender: Tip the bartender outrageously well when he or she serves you your first drink. Not only will this ensure that you are served quickly next time, but it always increases the odds that your next drink will be complimentary.

The "Oops" Factor: Sip your cocktail until it is almost gone, then, double-checking that you are directly in the bartender's line of sight, have your friend "bump" into you, spilling the remainder of your drink. Chances are the person behind the bar will give you a fresh one free of charge.

The Other "Oops" Factor: Again, with your cocktail almost totally depleted, stumble into an unsuspecting male, purposefully spilling the remainder of your drink (which should be mostly ice) all over the floor. The chivalry gene that most men still possess tells us that your marked man will probably freshen up your glass for you.

The Lean-In: All right, all right. We may be women of the new millennium, but we still think it's OK to use our, um, assets to get a free drink or two every once in a while, but we do not by any means make a habit of it. In fact, you should only use the lean-in when the situation is dire, such as if you had just slapped your ex across the face for a nasty comment, or all your martini money has disappeared. The lean-in is simple—you probably do it all the time and don't even notice. But if you need some instruction, follow these four easy steps:

1. Find your nearest male bartender.

2. Cross your arms underneath your cha-chas.

3. Slightly *lean in* across the bar as you order your drink.

4. Sip and enjoy your free cocktail!

So when a new club opening pops up on your calendar, throw on your most dazzling half-and-half ensemble, grab your well-stocked clutch bag, and review your Diva tricks of the trade. It's time to get your club on—Diva-style. Lexi probably put it best when she said, "To be a Social Diva, you have to be like the Confucius of club-going: you simply know all!"

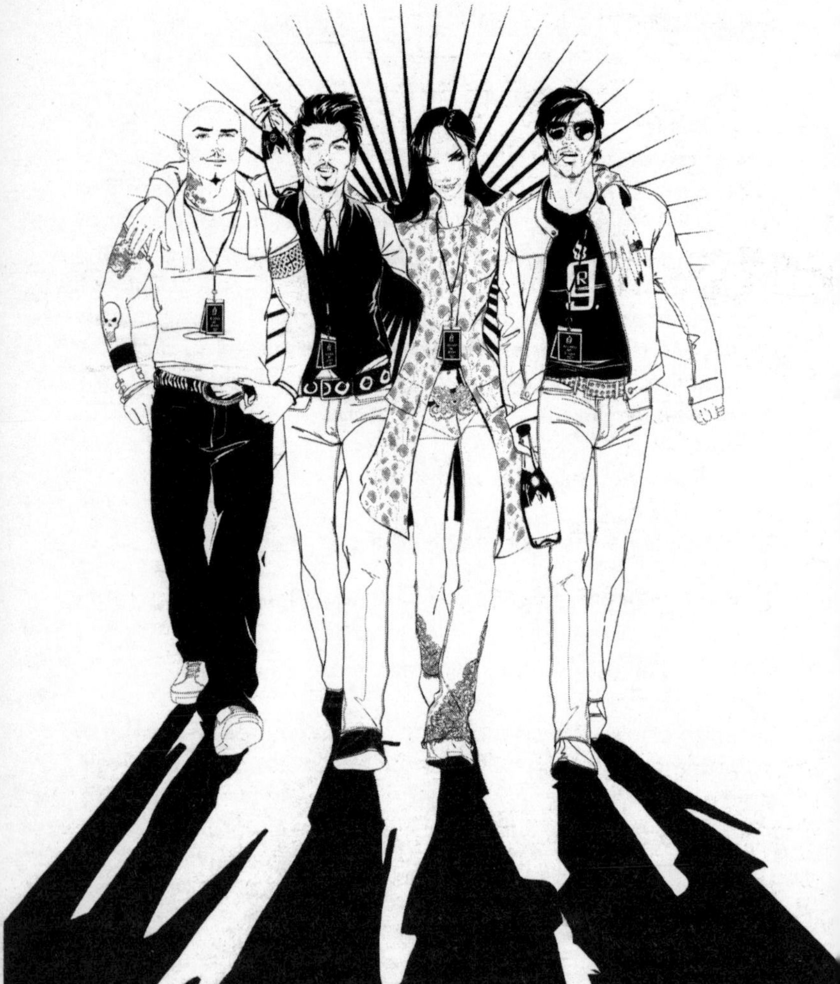

Chapter Nine

PARTY LIKE A ROCK STAR...
LITERALLY

How a Social Diva Does a Concert

It's Friday night and you have tickets to your favorite band's sold-out show. You're elated, and rightfully so, but suddenly Diva problems come to mind as you anticipate rocking out with the crowd: Should I wear heels or flats? What do I *have* to take in my bag? When choosing an outfit, should I channel Joan Jett or Gwen Stefani? What if I end up backstage? It's dizzying, we know, but the more you mull it over, the more rock time you're wasting, so let's get to it!

The first thing a Diva must do is to assess the type of concert you are about to attend. This will give you a good idea of who your style icon should be for the evening, and what shoes should adorn your pretty little feet.

Putting On The Right Style

GENRE	STYLE ICONS	THE BASICS
Rock	Debbie Harry Joan Jett	Lots of black; skinny jeans in dark denim; white tank top.
Punk	Siouxsie Sioux, Nancy Spungen	Loud or neon pops of color; black; arm warmers or fingerless gloves.
Country	Taylor Swift, The Dixie Chicks	Denim, and lots of it. And please don't wear anything fringed. It was not OK in the '80s, and soooo not OK now.
Pop	Gwen Stefani, Katy Perry	Anything trendy! When it comes to dressing for a pop concert, you can pretty much get away with anything you've seen listed as trend-worthy in your favorite gossip magazine.
Hip-Hop/Rap	Mary J. Blige, Fergie	Bottoms that show off your, um, well, bottom. No super-baggy trousers, Divas—those are strictly for the gentlemen.

THE EXTRAS	THE SHOES
Piles of silver jewelry, but nothing you would be devastated losing.	Black boots are a must, but they must have stacked heels—more comfortable than stilettos if you end up having to stand for the entire show.
Gothic Lolita adornments, such as earrings with dangling red plastic pistols, or frilled socks.	Classic Converse—any color or style that matches your look.
A leather belt with a cute buckle. They're not expensive, and they come in all kinds of styles, allowing you to inject a bit of your personality into your look.	We suggest a brown suede mid-calf boot with a stacked heel as an alternative to other, more predictable cowboy kicks. But if you must wear cowboy boots, buy them at Nordstrom, not Ed's Boot & Hat Emporium. We hope you understand the difference.
One of those fun little money-belt numbers is small enough to pose as an accessory, but large enough to eliminate the need for a bag. It's fabulous and functional. Hooray!	Your trendy outfit should be paired with pointy-toed, high-heeled shoes (bad news for your feet in this kind of situation). So you can either grit your teeth and wear your toe-killers, or pray that Rihanna is on the cover of this month's Vogue wearing flats.
A fedora hat. Nothing is hotter than a lady who can work it like a pimp, so stick a feather in your cap (literally) and rock it!	You have the same dilemma here as you did at the pop concert because heels are usually the "it" shoe for this kind of show. Try something with a platform and square toe; they can be more comfortable than other high-heeled shoes, and more stable than designs without a platform.

Four Steps to a Bagless Existence

After you've achieved victory over the daunting task of figuring out what to wear, it's time to decide what you need to take along with you—and how on earth you're going to carry it!

First off, taking a bag into a concert is usually a bad idea, especially if your ticket is a general admission floor seat or if you plan on standing during the majority of the show (trust us, you're not going to need any extra weight when you're trying to balance in those heels). We know it sounds crazy, but there are effective ways to take all your essentials into a concert without having to carry them in a huge bag. And without further ado, here they are.

1. The Car Bag
The car bag is like your concert first-aid kit, and will remain in your parked vehicle. It holds all the essential items you will need post-concert and pre-after-party.

If you live in a big city and plan to take a cab, train, or bus to your concert destination, put on some old-school style and rent a locker at the venue. Larger venues typically have some sort of system you can use to lock up your valuables, and at an incredibly cheap price. Invest the money and lock up your Birkin…you don't want to be the girl smacking everyone in the face with your huge bag all night, right?

CAR BAG CONTENTS
- Travel-sized deodorant—you will need it once the concert is over

- Travel-size packet of Wet Wipes—to remove any perspiration that may have occurred during the show, and destroy any germs left behind from the ladies' room

- Small bottle of mouthwash—to eliminate the post-concert beer breath

- Small bottle of aspirin or ibuprofen—just in case you were standing a little too close to the speakers

2. The Concert Essentials Bag

This bag should be small enough to fit inside your car bag, but large enough to hold all your essential items. Remembering what these essentials are is super-easy because there are only four must-haves for any concert (besides your ticket of course). Just remember the acronym MILK.

M = Money
I = Identification
L = Lip gloss/lipstick
K = Keys

Simple! Now, you might want to take a few extra items with you in case of emergency. For example, your cell phone might be a good idea in the event that you and your fellow concert-goers are separated. Plus, most cells come equipped with cameras, and how awesome would it be to capture the moment when you meet the band backstage? Um, pretty awesome!

3. Upon Arrival

When you get to the concert venue, park your car and go through the following procedure:

- Remove the concert essentials bag from the car bag.

- Your money and ID are the most important items you're taking in with you, so store them in a place where you'll *definitely* notice if someone tries to steal them even if you're distracted by the lead singer licking his microphone. We suggest your bra. Secure these items in one of the cups, not under the elastic band that goes around your chest. We've tested it both ways and found that things move around too much under the band and, after about an hour, can be quite uncomfortable.

- Your lip gloss/lipstick can go into one of your pockets (if you have any), or conceal it in your sock or boot.

- As for your keys, detach your car key from your key ring. Put all your remaining keys in your car bag so that you can easily access them later. Now you can lock and unlock your vehicle, and have to hide only one key (instead of that massive key ring) on your person. You can put it in your pocket (if you have one); you can thread a chain through it and wear it as a necklace, à la Janet Jackson circa 1987, or you can put Lexi's trick into practice.

LEXI'S PATENT-PENDING KEY TRICK

 Keep your car key on its own key ring and attach the ring to the belt loop on your jeans or pants. Now put on your belt and tuck your dangling key underneath it. Ta-daa! A hidden key that cannot get lost!

- If you need to keep your phone with you, it's usually best to hide it in your back pocket. But if you have no back pockets, the waistband of your pants is usually pretty effective. Another option is the very center of your bra, where your breasts separate. Most phones fit in there perfectly! Whichever place you choose, put your phone into a case that has some sort of clip to help keep it secure.

4. The Final Assessment of the Goods

Don't keep anything of great importance (i.e., your Jimmy Choos or a wallet full of credit cards) in your car bag. Second, store your car bag in the trunk so that it is completely hidden from passersby. You don't want to encourage an opportunist thief to smash your window and grab your car bag off the seat. The fool might only get away with some mouthwash and deodorant, but you still have a shattered window to fix, and that is a drama a Diva does not need. Before you walk away from your car, make one last assessment of your car bag and ask yourself: "Is there anything in here that is irreplaceable, extremely expensive, or would cause me a great deal of unnecessary angst if it were stolen?" If the answer is "no," close the trunk, lock the car, and proceed inside to rock out. If the answer is "yes," go back to step 1.

Storm the Backstage!

You've got the look, the shoes, and your strategically hidden concert essentials down, so now it's time to plan your backstage attack (because we know you've already scored backstage passes, you sassy Diva, you!). Top of the list is to finagle your after-party invitation, and, of course, your favorite rock star's phone number…all in a matter of twenty-five minutes. Sounds impossible? Not if you're a Social Diva!

Beat the crowd

Go backstage right before the headliner's encore. We know, we know—if you go backstage at that time, you'll miss your favorite song. But ask yourself this, Diva: Do you want to hear your favorite song for the billionth time or meet the artist who wrote it? You'll beat out the rest of the backstage pass-holders by about fifteen minutes, ensuring that you'll be one of the first in line for post-set autographs. Plus, it's almost guaranteed that the opening act will still be hanging out by the catering table, so you'll get a chance to chat with an up-and-coming band (and gain bragging rights with your friends when these bands hit it big later).

Place Yourself Accordingly

When the band comes offstage, position yourself so that you're in their sightline, though not too close. You don't want to crowd them, or be mistaken for a groupie; you just want to be close enough to be noticeable, and let them come to you.

Start Chatting

To get an invite to the super-exclusive after-party, or score a band member's number, you have to establish some sort of relationship. The best way to do that is by being your charming, witty, delightful self in conversation. However, before you start flirting with one of these tattooed and leather-clad fellows, you need to work out who is the most promising target. Thus, we've compiled this handy guide to help you decide which band member is right for you, and how to nab him.

HOW TO CHOOSE MR. RIGHT BAND MEMBER

Lead Singer

How to spot one: Tight pants, eyeliner, surrounded by women with fake breasts and collagen injections.

How to bag one: Don't talk to him at all. Seriously, if you keep your distance, he's sure to notice you simply because you're the only woman in the room who's not fawning over him. And since it is the foremost job of the frontman to get everyone to like both him and his band, he'll be on a mission for your attention.

Pros: He can sing and (most likely) write songs, which means you have a pretty decent chance that he'll write a song about you. I mean, come on, how awesome would it be to join the ranks of Roxanne, Mandy, and Peggy Sue? Additionally, he has a fabulous wardrobe, better shoes than you, and makes ideal arm candy for photographs.

145

Cons:	He gets the most attention from the press, the fans, and, most notably, the groupies. This means that you'll have to deal with an overabundance of scantily clad, Aquanet avengers, along with his oversized ego.
Conclusion:	If you have the courage to put him in his place every once in a while, and a killer right hook (for the groupies, of course), you can totally date a lead singer.
Boyfriend rating:	C. Originally, the lead singer received a D on the Social Diva Boyfriend Rating Scale, since a true Diva can't stand the fact that he gets more attention, and has a better shoe collection. But considering that we might be forever commemorated on an album just for dating him, we had to give him a few extra points.
Our favorites:	Jon Bon Jovi—for the hair. David Bowie—for inventing glam rock. Mick Jagger—for the lips and the signature dance moves. Sting—can anyone say tantric sex? (um, because we surely can!)

Lead Guitarist

How to spot one:	Has longer hair than you, calluses on his fingers, a shot of whisky in one hand and a cigarette in the other.
How to bag one:	Tell him that he's as skillful as Peter Frampton. Trust us. It works.

Pros:	Typically, the lead guitarist is the one who writes the music part of the songs, which means he's creative, deep, and very talented. Moreover, the high-kick spin move he unleashes when he solos indicates an intensity that usually makes an encore in the bedroom.
Cons:	If he's any good, he probably gets as much attention as the lead singer (think Eddie Van Halen), and this leads to the same relationship pitfalls that you would have with the frontman.
Conclusion:	If you're familiar with the Kama Sutra, have an affection for calloused fingertips, and the same kind of right hook as the lead singer's girlfriend, the lead guitarist is your guy.
Boyfriend rating:	B-. We had to knock off some points because we might have to destroy some eighteen-year-old girl's buy-one-get-one-free boob job to ensure some security in the relationship.
Our favorites:	Keith Richards—for retaining his style over the past hundred years. Dave Navarro—for wearing more eyeliner than we do, and still looking hot. Slash—for keeping the top hat, no matter what the fashionistas say.

Bassist

How to spot one   Shy disposition offstage and lack of a guitar pick; probably wearing the same outfit he wore at his day job.

How to bag one: You'll have to approach him, because he's too shy to come on to you. Open the conversation by talking about how much you love your new Stevie Wonder greatest hits album. Most bassists, even the ones in hardcore rock bands, love funk music from the '70s because of its bass-heavy sound.

Pros: The bassist is typically "above the hype." He is totally used to the lead singer and the lead guitarist getting all the attention, but he really doesn't mind. So it's safe to assume that he'll allow you to be the center of attention in the relationship (which you know you love, Diva!).

Cons: All the other Divas are going to want to date him after they read this.

Conclusion: If you love attention, Sly and the Family Stone, and have the mental muscle to outwit a few other Divas, then the bassist is your man.

Boyfriend rating: A. This guy is the man that every Diva needs in her life: someone who is quiet enough to allow her to talk incessantly about the new Prada line, but has a big enough personality to hold his own—onstage and with you at any shindig.

Our favorites:	Flea—for infamously rocking the sweat sock.
	Paul McCartney—for being the cutest Beatle.
	Gene Simmons—for obvious reasons.

Drummer

How to spot one   He'll be shirtless, no question. It gets mighty warm behind those drum sets, you know.

How to bag one: In order to bag a drummer, you need only say two words: Neil Peart. When you ask a drummer who his inspiration/idol is, he will without a doubt name the man who banged the drums for Rush, and will be incredibly impressed that you even know who he is.

Pros: Typically, the drummer will have a killer upper body because he (obviously) bangs away on his kit all day. He'll also have the best sense of humor and be the friendliest out of all the band members. (Because drummers are usually placed near the back of the stage, to get noticed they have to have twice as much charisma as the other guys.)

Cons: The constant tapping. A real drummer plays all day, every day, the only variable being what he's actually playing on. You know that kid who sat behind you in Math and tapped his pencil on the desk for the duration of the class? He's a drummer. Also, drummers have been known to have anger management issues, which is usually why they chose to drum in the first place—to blow off some steam.

Conclusion   If you like intensity, find bicep definition extremely sexy, and own shares in an aspirin company, go get yourself a drummer.

Boyfriend rating: B+. Divas love a man with a great sense of humor and a big personality (just as long as it doesn't overshadow hers). Plus, the drummer's characteristics will make him an excellent partner for all the parties you must attend. The only thing that brings him down from an A is that incessant tapping thing— it's nothing personal.

Our favorites: Neil Peart—for getting us so many dates with other drummers.

Tommy Lee—for performing on a high-flying, rotating drum kit.

Animal (from *The Muppet Show*)—for gloriously chanting "Woman! Woman!"

So you see, Diva, once you stop beating around the amplifier, pick your style icon, stash your belongings in your bra, and get your fabulous self backstage, the lead guitarist's phone number is only a mention of "Frampton" away.

And that, ladies, is how a Social Diva does a concert!

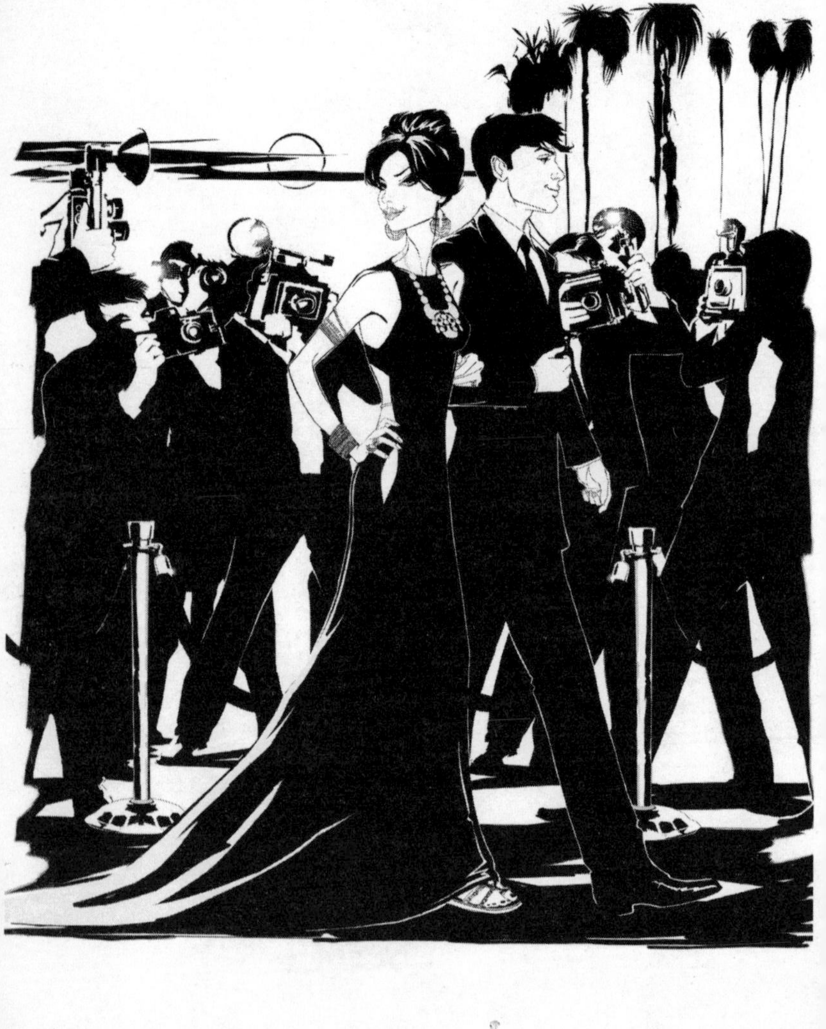

Chapter Ten

THE HOLY GRAIL

How a Social Diva Does the Red Carpet

So, Diva, let's say you hit the jackpot of all jackpots and get the chance to (gasp!) *walk the red carpet.*

After reveling in this, the most amazing and fabulous news you ever received in your entire existence, you surface from Cloud Nine and exclaim, "Oh, my God! What the *@!* am I going to wear? I still need to lose the weight I gained during the holidays! But more important, what shoes shall I wear?"

Okay, Diva, first things first...Breathe! It's all good! The gods of fabulous social soirées have descended on your ever-so-deserving social life and things are about to happen in a major way. Now let's get moving!

The Social Diva Pre-Show

Now that you've had a chance to collect yourself after the initial shock, we suggest that you make a detailed timetable leading up to the day of the big event. Work backwards from your end date, scheduling your various salon and spa appointments, along with some extra sessions with your personal trainer, and start your hunt for that perfect red carpet–worthy dress. Even if you have only three days, Diva, you are savvy enough to set yourself up to be a "Best" (not a "Worst").

The Body
Start pumping those weights to ensure that your arms look toned in your sensational off-the-shoulder number. Get a personal trainer and hit the gym in a serious way. Time to make that New Year's resolution (you know, the one you've made every year since you can remember) a reality. Even with only a few days to prepare, fitting in some hard-core workouts and sticking to the right diet can help you look and feel your best.

Need even more motivation to get on the elliptical? How about this: TV cameras add ten pounds to your appearance, and those pesky flat-screen TVs can make women who wear a size 2 look as big as a house!

This is not to say you are not already beautiful, and we certainly don't want you developing an eating disorder. But all Divas know that a healthy diet and exercise are good things, and what better excuse to get in the spirit of them than a red carpet event? Think about it this way: say you're at work, or a restaurant, or a coffee shop, and someone asks if you want dessert or a pastry and you'll have the opportunity to respond, "Oh, I'm sorry, but I can't order dessert! The Oscars are coming up, and you know television adds ten pounds." What could be more Diva than that?

ANOTHER PERK!

 Exercise will not only help you work off all that extra adrenaline you're pumping, it will also improve your sleep. Divas absolutely must get their beauty sleep before big events to keep up with those A-listers who party till dawn!

The Dress

OK, now that you're working out and eating right, it's time to think about an outfit. And we're not just talking about any old ensemble. We're talking about the dress to put all other dresses to utter shame. A dress that makes you feel totally glam, photographs well, and looks hot on TV.

Don't have the bucks to drop on the latest Versace number? Do as the celebs do: borrow and promote. Perhaps you might not be acquainted with Donatella (a Diva among Divas), but by this point in our book, you know that up-and-coming designers are a must for your contacts list, and now is the time to put in the call. Simply let him or her know that you have been invited to a seriously A-list event, and you were hoping you could borrow something absolutely fabulous. In return, when reporters ask, "Who are you wearing?" your new best friend (a.k.a your up-and-coming designer pal) will get some free publicity. Plus, if the designer gets some press coverage after you work those clothes down the red carpet, then he or she will doubtless adorn you with many more goodies for your closet. And that, Divas, is what we call a WWD—Win-Win Diva-style!

No couturier on call? Go vintage. Simply call all your favorite local vintage shops, share the news, and ask if they have anything on their racks that would suit the occasion. If their stock is devoid of red carpet–worthy frocks, ask if they could please keep a watchful eye out on your behalf.

Still striking out? Black is the new black! You will definitely find a red carpet–suitable black dress for under $400, and with those newly toned arms of yours (you *are* working out, right, Diva?), you will look terrific! Donna Karen, Calvin Klein, and ABS by Allen Schwartz are all carry carpet-worthy frocks that will have you looking lovely without sending you to credit card hell (and help you to save some cash for shoes).

The Shoes
Speaking of shoes (our favorite topic!), what better excuse is there to buy a new pair of Jimmy Choos than a red carpet event? The right pair of shoes can make any outfit look like it cost a million bucks. So even if you have to succumb to a budget on your dress, splurge on the heels—it will be well worth it when your little tootsies are featured in next month's *Vogue*.

The Baubles
Once you have the "look," it's time to choose adornments. But how do you look super-duper fab without 300 carats of bling? Well, if you aren't close enough with Harry Winston to borrow some precious gems, there is no shame in going faux. Cubic

zirconiums are so good these days that unless you're a certified jeweler you can barely tell the difference between them and real diamonds. Austrian crystal is another sparkly option to consider. Check out celebrity- and designer-inspired jewels on websites like www.emitations.com. It's a low-cost way to achieve the closest thing to designer style.

The Unseen

Now that you are all glam on the exterior, it's time to focus on what's happening underneath your dress. You definitely don't want to have a Tara Reid moment on the red carpet, so keeping that dress in place is imperative, Diva! To work it à la J-Lo in her infamously low-cut Versace, employ the help of some double-sided tape. For this, we highly recommend Hollywood Fashion Tape, which is specifically designed to gently bond your skin to your garment. It's much better than double-sided Scotch tape, and doesn't hurt to pull off.

But ensuring that your bosoms are safe and secure is not the only issue to consider when shopping for red carpet undergarments. You also want to purchase items that will flatten out any unwanted curves, eliminate panty lines, and, most important, make your tush look its most fabulous! Hit your local lingerie store and consult a saleswoman: she should be able to help you find just what you need to suit your body's special needs. And remember Diva, Spanx by Sara Blakely are a red-carpet walkers' best friend!

DEFINITE RED CARPET DON'T

Unless you are a pop star, don't get too outrageous with your ensemble. This will not get you noticed (well, at least not in a good way). Instead it will get you whispered about behind your back, if not laughed at in your face. We are serious, Diva. The reason pop-star Divas can be so daring with their wardrobe choices is because their main objective is to get some ink. For them, any press is good press, and they usually have the vocal chords to back it up. Moreover, Social Divas are never fashion victims, so always keep it classy, ladies!

All right, Diva, you've got the body, you've got the dress, and you've got *The Shoes*. Now you are officially ready to make the necessary pre-event arrangements.

The Primp

Hair and makeup appointments are a must. They are red carpet weapons and major stress relievers. Professional styling guarantees that you're going to look fabulous all night, freeing you to focus on more important things, such as how you're going to mingle your way into the hottest after-party. It's also a smart idea to book run-through appointments with your stylists so that you can be sure you'll be completely satisfied with your look, pre-flashbulbs.

OUT-OF-TOWN STYLING

Is the event in a city other than your hometown? Ask your local stylist to take digital photos of you in your pre-approved look. Then take the photos with you to your destination salon so you can show them concrete examples of exactly what you want.

Hair up or down? Depends on the dress, the jewelry, and the overall look you're going for. Wearing your locks up is generally more glam, so if your dress suggests a 1950s Hollywood starlet, we would advise sticking with an up-do. If your dress is low-cut, wear your mane down, as it complements the plunging neckline. The goal here, Diva, is to frame your lovely face so that when someone (or the camera) looks you up and down, you look breathtaking!

TIME IT RIGHT

Make sure you give yourself plenty of time to get ready, and don't stay out too late the night before. You want to be fresh and ready for your event (and the after-party).

Show Time!

The limo pulls up, the doors open…and this is *it*, Diva! Take a deep breath, step out of the car (being careful to avoid any Britney Spears moments), and smile for the camera.

The scene is typically quite chaotic: hordes of celebs, photographers, camera crews, PR reps (a.k.a. "handlers"), and, of course, the onlookers who wish they were you.

When it comes to walking the red carpet, the handlers control the flow. They are usually the ones who decide which crew or photog gets to interview or photograph the celebs and industry peeps. These same handlers will walk you through what you need to do, where you need to stop, and where you need to wait. All you have to do is follow their instructions, smile, and be gorgeous!

Keeping It Diva

At the best red carpet affairs you could be surrounded by A-listers, and the last thing you want to do is to look like a newbie. On the red carpet you must take the cues from your handler and keep moving, even though you are dying inside because you just spotted Gerard Butler (we would be, too). But you have to hold it in! You won't explode, instead you will radiate Diva-ness from all the excitement.

When working the red carpet, you must watch, listen, and follow. In unfamiliar situations the key is never to look uncomfortable, so no fidgeting or panicked glances, Diva.

If you do get into a conversation, keep it light. Compliments work best and usually get returned. After about three or four sets of kind words from your fellow carpet walkers, you'll be glowing and smiling so much that you'll feel like you're in heaven—well, in a Social Diva's heaven anyway!

No Gawking or Stalking

Didn't your mother tell you it was impolite to stare? Let's say you're strutting your stuff down the carpet, and when you look up your favorite celeb is right next to you. What do you do, Diva?

We think it is acceptable to say hello and how much you like his or her work. You cannot, simply *cannot*, shriek, shrill, or gawk.

For example, let's say that this favorite celeb of yours is Kim

Cattrall (because you simply loved her in *Sex and the City*). You can say something like, "Your performance in *Sex and the City* was fabulous, well done! I enjoyed it very much." You *cannot* say, "Oh, my God! Kim Cattrall! Smith—your boyfriend in *SATC*—was *sooo* hot!" Gushing like that won't get you any kind of real conversation or get you invited to the after-party.

The same goes for male actors. It's tempting when Dr. McDreamy is right in front of you, but keep your excitement to yourself. Remember, Diva, you have to appear as though you attend these events all the time. Social Divas must never be labeled "stalker-azzi!"

Say Brie!

Ready for some lights, cameras, action? Lots of potential photo opportunities will come your way when walking the red carpet, and a Social Diva knows exactly when to make the picture-perfect pose that can hit all the celeb-style magazines.

Spotting a Photo Op
The first photo opportunity you'll discover on your walk down the red carpet is the sponsorship wall (the "step and repeat," as industry insiders call it), which is, essentially, a white backdrop covered in the event sponsor's logos. You've probably seen this wall before, as this is where a lot of the pictures you see in gossip rags are taken. As the cameras flash away, you and your date should look from side to side, not directly into the flash. We don't want you blinded for the remainder of your red carpet experience!

STEP ON THE "T"

 At every red carpet event there will be masking tape on the floor (usually in the shape of a T), indicating where you need to stop in order to be properly photographed.

The Rita Wilson Maneuver

If your date is famous (and you're, well, not as famous), but you are so wanting to get in the next issue of *Us Weekly*, pull the Rita Wilson Maneuver.

What *is* the Rita Wilson Maneuver, you ask? Well, when the divine Miss Wilson was still an up-and-coming starlet and attending high-class functions with her then-boyfriend Tom Hanks, she would always make sure that her face was touching his any time a shutterbug was taking his picture. This little move made it virtually impossible for photo editors to cut her out of the frame. And largely because of her savvy technique, she became known in her own right.

The Perfect Pose

If posing alone, use the classic over-the-shoulder turn. Stand still and twist to the left, angling your head over your shoulder, with your chin down (not too far down—you don't want a double chin). To top it all off, place your left hand on your hip so that your arm points away from your body. This pose makes celebs look lean and complements a lovely dress at the same time. If executed properly, the photogs will think *you* are the next up-and-coming starlet—hey, a Diva can dream, can't she? Practice, practice, practice this pose in front of a mirror, and have a Diva friend take digitals to ensure you have the pose down pat for the big day.

On the Inside

Once you've strutted your Diva stuff on the red carpet, it's time to find your seat inside the venue. Chances are you will have a slew of celebs around you. And if you're there as the date of someone who is nominated, you will be mingling with the A-list! This means maximum opportunity to have your pretty mug plastered all over the TV along with the rest of the starlets.

During the award ceremony stay alert and looking your best, especially when you see a camera nearby: chances are high that they are going to shoot people at your table or in your row. Award shows love to reveal the glitz and glam in the seats as well as onstage. Before the camera draws in, make sure you are sitting up straight and looking fantastic (this is not the time to take a peek in a mirror or reapply lip gloss).

NO TOOTH-PICKING ALLOWED

If the cameras are near and you're worried that you might have something on your teeth, do not attempt to pick the foreign item out of your mouth. Instead, you should smile without showing those pearly whites: we promise you'll still look amazing!

PACE YOURSELF

Most award shows are very, very long. If you are cocktailing, pace yourself, Diva! You don't want to say something crazy or pass out before they announce Best Picture. Plus, there will be many after-parties to attend, and you don't want to miss one second of this evening above all evenings!

And the Winner Is...

During the nomination process, you must clap after each name is called—it is just proper and polite. Only a light clap is necessary. You'll be doing a *lot* of clapping throughout the night, and you don't want your hands to ache at the after-party.

If someone at your table or sitting nearby is nominated, clapping a little harder is pretty much required. Leave hooting and hollering to the A-listers (they're allowed). Be excited but remain sophisticated, Diva.

KEEP SMILING

Never ever make disapproving faces. Some cameras are farther away than others and you never know when you're being included in a shot. You don't want them catching you frowning, right, Diva?

Once the winner is announced, it is, of course, mandatory to clap. But keep in mind a few lesser-known guidelines. If someone at your table or in your row wins, for instance, it is appropriate to say congratulations as they head up to receive. Additionally, if the people at your table or in your row initiate a standing ovation, you should follow suit. And finally, if a huge award is being presented (anything with "Best" in front of it), or the winner of the award is considered a legend (e.g., Judi Dench or Sean Connery), a standing ovation is de rigueur.

STANDING ROOM ONLY

If someone sitting next to you or at your table wins, this is doubly exciting because—to the cameras—it will appear that you belong to one of the "it" groups. And that equals more camera time, Diva!

Now that you know how to work the red carpet like an A-lister, you'll be ready and confident when someone asks you to be their plus one at the Cannes Film Festival. And remember, Diva, when it comes to the red carpet, you have to work it to own it!

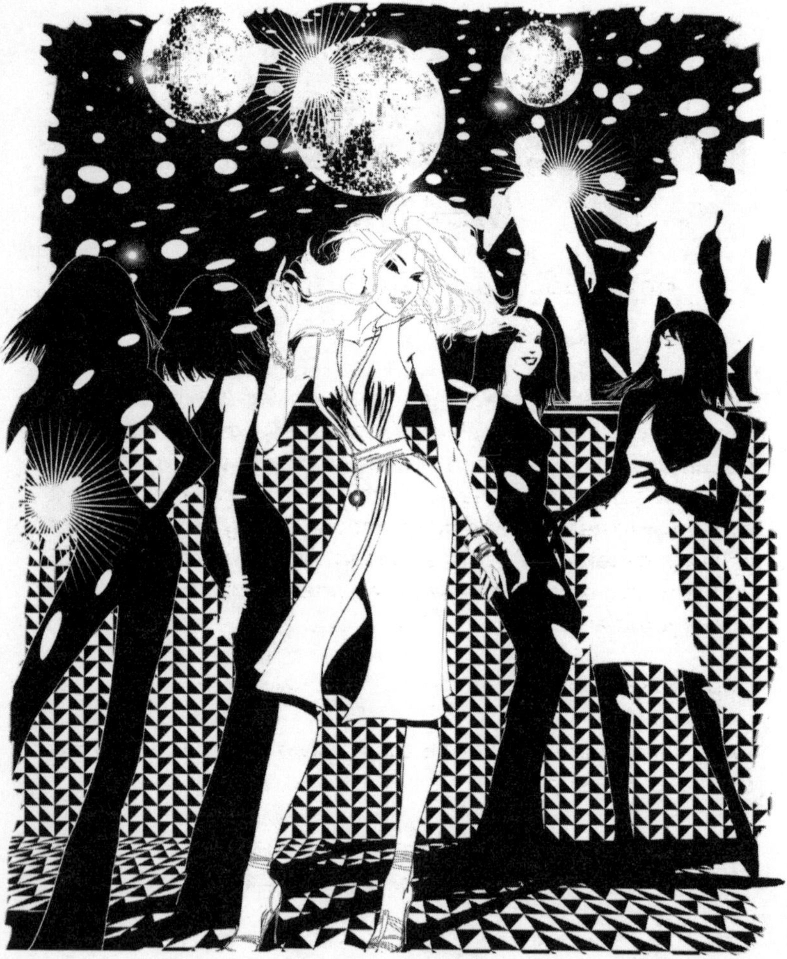

Chapter Eleven

DIVAS GIVE FASHIONABLY LATE A WHOLE NEW MEANING

How a Social Diva Does an After-Party

Sometimes a Social Diva wants to stay out past her bedtime. Whether last call is early—or just too early for you, night-owl Diva—why not go out and play more? For example, let's say you're at a black-tie benefit, which, as we've established, is a super way to network and do something for a good cause, and you're (maybe) getting a little sauced. At that point you realize that you have done all the work you need to do and you'd like to get your party on.

What to do, what to do?

Well, Diva, there's only one thing more fun than the main event—the after-party!

So when going home is not a desirable option, grab your close friends and get to it! It's time to after-party, Diva-style.

REFRAIN AND RETAIN

If you are going out after hours, do your drinking at the end of the initial party. Peg, although she has a liver of steel, will refrain from cocktailing until the event is practically over. Yes, she's got a drink in her hand, in super-social mode, but she is too busy chatting and making sure everything is going according to plan to waste time downing cocktails.

Where's the Party?

Diva, know that there is *always* an after-party; you just need to know where to look. If you are not at an award show (where after-parties are so standard that you would have to be deaf and blind to miss your invite), or you're not part of the in-crowd at a new club in town, here's how to find the hottest happening after-hours bashes.

Word of mouth. Generally, there is someone buzzing around telling the cool crowd what is going on afterward. Keep your eyes open for that hipster host and the rest will fall into place.

Ask the staff. You should already be tipping the bartender well (remember what we said about tipping?), so asking is easy. Another person with a wealth of information on every hot spot is the DJ. He'll know everything that's going on. He could be booked to spin after hours at a different venue, so you could just roll in with him. "I'm with the DJ" always works to get in as a VIP!

Find a friend in PR. Keep the public relations reps in your address book up to date! We mentioned earlier that PR people can help you get a table at a top-notch restaurant, but in an awards situation they can do so much more. See, Diva, PR reps live for being in the know—it's what they get paid for—so they can be your go-to pals for getting the scoop on what's happening after a big event.

DO YOUR HOMEWORK, DIVA!

To get into an after-party you can refer back to chapter 8 about club-hopping (see "Getting Past the Gatekeeper" on page 129). The same rules really do apply, mostly because after-parties tend to be held at clubs.

Hmm, Where to Go, Where to Go?

Once you know (or if you already knew) all the hip and fabulous places in the city, your main concern is working out which place is hosting the best party.

Cut-Throughs

Location, location, location! Just like property, the hottest venues always attract the hottest crowds, no matter what the proximity to the original venue. Don't deceive yourself into thinking that a venue close to the main event might be a better after-party. Parties close to the initial event venue should be considered "cut-throughs," a term Peg and her friends have given to a party that has to be checked out while en route to the final destination.

DON'T WASTE PARTY TIME

When visiting a cut-through, take a quick walk around the venue to decide whether it's worth your time to grab a drink and hang out for a while before moving on. Don't make the bar your first stop. If you get a cocktail and the vibe at the bar is lame, you're stuck there until you finish your drink, wasting valuable party time!

If the venue in question is near a big-time event (i.e., a fashion or award show), it is probably worth a look no matter what. Chances are you will see quite a few celebs who want to get an obligatory post-awards show cocktail before they have to go home and hit the hay for an early call time. Those really into partying will be at the hip locale. And since you don't want to be the first ones at the hip and fabulous after-party, you have some time to kill anyway.

The Awards Show After-Party

When is an after-party better than the main event? When it's after an award show, especially if you had lousy seats. If you find yourself seated in nosebleed, there is little reason for your fabulous self to sit through the entire show, because you'll never get on camera. But tough it out, Diva, because nothing is more fun than heading out afterward and hanging with the celebs (who are now more relaxed because the ceremony is over).

The Fashion Show After-Party

Fashion show after-parties are always a must because they're full of people who are notorious for doing nothing but partying. They are beautiful and dressed to catwalk perfection, so why wouldn't they want to go out? London, Milan, New York, Paris are where the main fashion shows take place, and these are the main events for a Social Diva.

The best after-parties are for the most well-known designers and the best of the up-and-coming ones. The shows are meant to present the couture and gain publicity for the line, and just as it's important to fill the front rows with key media people, celebrities and other noteworthy types, it's also important to have an amazing after-party bash. The after-party entices more A-listers and ensures that the couture house *keeps* getting talked about.

Other Late Nights

No award shows or fashion events in your town? Everything closed or lame, with no cool spot on your horizon? Don't despair—just get spontaneous and put something together yourself.

Spontaneous After-Party
You don't have to go home, but you can't stay all night at the venue! When the bars or clubs close some night owls love to host after-hours parties as much as they like to be entertained, so decide whose apartment is best for late-night fun and head over there. The first thing to consider when choosing a place is the noise factor. If the hostess has crusty old neighbors who hit the ceiling with a broom when the TV is too loud, chances are this is not the best place to throw your swinging after-party. Other factors to consider are who has the best sound system and music collection (which may not matter, as long as you

take your iPod, as we taught you), who has the best space to accommodate all the guests; and whose place has the booze!

If the best party pad and the abundance of spirits are not in the same locale (and they never are, Diva), then it is time to do some quick party logistics and divide the responsibilities. Send only two people to buy alcohol and mixers at the nearest liquor store. More people than that and it's a committee that will never reach any decisions. Send the rest of your crew over to the party pad to prep it for the fun time ahead!

You never know, Diva, with your help your friend's party pad might turn out to be the newest hot spot in town. A friend of Peg's named Jay had an apartment that was so popular for entertaining after hours that it became known around the club circuit as Club J, and some people thought it was a real, honest-to-goodness venue.

DIY After-Party

Why not create your own after-party? You are a Social Diva, after all. Perhaps you're deterred by past experiences when your best shot at party time didn't work out and everything turned into a stress-fest, or even something merely (gasp) so-so. Maybe you made the mistake of inviting your boss or C-listers, which meant you couldn't completely relax and have a good time because you had to watch yourself or watch others. Or perhaps your brother, who is in a nasty fight with your best friend, insisted on coming and you ended up playing referee all night? That's a recipe for disaster.

As a true Social Diva, you know your evening isn't dead until the sun comes up, so here's how to get your party on. Be a sly Diva and text or phone your chosen guests from the privacy of the ladies' room. No unwanted types will know what you're up to as long as you're careful. And you'll feel terrific knowing that you're making your own Diva-style arrangements to after-party.

THREE MUST-HAVES FOR YOUR PERSONAL AFTER-PARTY

1. Limo. Letting someone else do the driving is always a treat. Even if you normally travel by trusty taxi, it is beyond fabulous to have transport just sitting outside waiting for you and your posse at all your destinations. So go ahead and splurge on a limo—you deserve it, Diva!

2. Alcohol. Champagne works remarkably well in limos because no mixers are required.

3. A-plus guest list. This consists of your non-drama Diva friends who just want to have a good party. A nice mixture of guys and girls (always more girls if you are hitting a club), and of course your super-Diva PR friend who can take responsibility for "What's going on after this?" out of your hands.

With these things in place, your work is done. It's now time to relax and have some much-needed fun.

After-Party Attire

Once you've grabbed your crew and made a plan, you need to decide if what you are wearing is appropriate for after hours, or whether you need to make a quick change.

Let's say, for example, you're at a black-tie event and want to head to a club. In this case an outfit change is required, otherwise you'll never get in, or you'll feel completely out of place. If you didn't plan ahead and your own place is completely out of the way, you can after-party in a posh hotel or restaurant bar, or even a members-only club (of course you belong to Soho House, Diva!) so that you and your crew can continue the evening without having to change clothes.

If you have time for a quick change, put on something totally fun. This is one instance when you can play up a trend or mix and match. If you want to be daring, go for it! Anything goes on the after-party circuit. Just avoid flashy pieces that others may recognize as coming off a discount department store rack (we're not saying *not* to wear something discounted—just make sure it's not recognizable as such). If your outfit is an unrecognizable piece and someone asks you where you bought it, you can always say you picked it up on your last trip to New York or Paris, or whatever fashionable city you're not in at the moment. This will generally glaze over the whole "Who is it by?" discussion.

PACK FOR GREATNESS

If you know you're going to be staying out late, Diva, it's wise to carry some items in your bag for freshening up. For this you'll need a bag that is a bit larger than a clutch but not as big as a day bag. In it you should be able to fit a small cosmetics bag containing the bare essentials. You also might want to include your big sunglasses in the case that the sun does indeed rise before you get home.

Stay up all night, play till dawn, but get home before the sun shines: that's how we do after-parties Diva-style!

BASIC AFTER-PARTY RULES

Wear something comfortable yet fashionable. Make sure your shoes can go the extra mile...literally! You will be walking around quite a bit, and nothing is more of a personal downer than sore feet.

Arrive no earlier than thirty to forty-five minutes after the party begins. You never want to be the first one there.

Talk to the host, or at least know who the host is.

Hang out in the hottest spot. This depends on where the party is being held. When at someone's house, head for the kitchen or the smoking section—wherever the action seems to be. At a club, seek out the VIP room, of course!

Leave before the sun comes up. It's always a good idea to get home before dawn, even on the biggest party nights. So make sure you are safely tucked into bed before you hear the birds chirping. You do need your beauty sleep, after all!

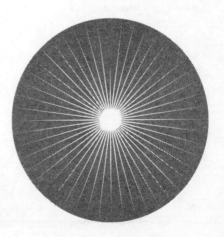

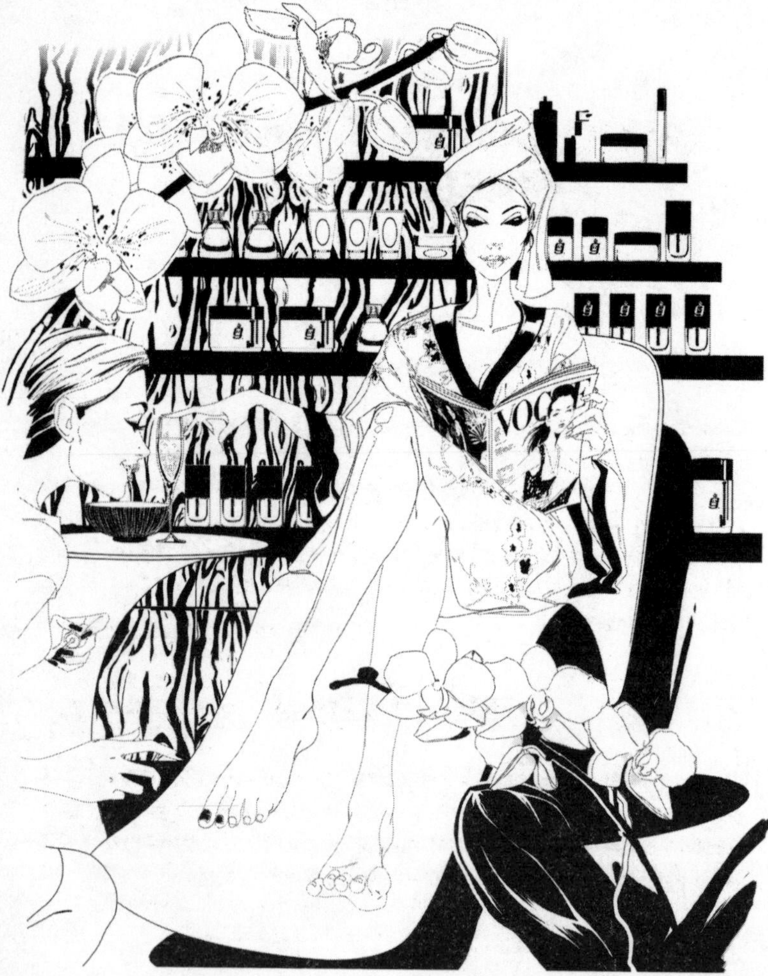
VOGUE

Chapter Twelve

WHO DOESN'T WANT TO MASSAGE ME?

How a Social Diva Does Rejuvenation

When living the Social Diva lifestyle to its fullest, even the most energetic and outgoing Divas need downtime to regroup, recharge, and renew. How do you do this? By hitting the spa of course! A quick treatment at a day spa or a totally secluded spa retreat should be part of any Diva's regular regime. You'll look amazing (as usual), and you'll be ready to hit the party circuit all over again.

What to Book

Not sure where to start? Just ask yourself whether you need some routine beauty maintenance, a massage to remove that knot in your back, or just some time to relax. Treatments are available to fix every bit of you from head to toe!

Men Have Their Cars,
Women Have Their Hair

Your hair maintenance schedule should include a cut, color, and the occasional deep-conditioning treatment when necessary. If you're not sure what your hair needs, schedule a consultation with an in-house senior stylist or colorist before you book. This ensures that you will get the right appointment with the proper treatment for your needs.

Diva, the only thing more crucial than what you do to your hair is who does it. We recommend having two different stylists: one who specializes in cutting and another who specializes in coloring. Although they have probably been trained in both skills, most stylists choose to focus on one in particular. Choosing professionals who specialize in one skill almost guarantees that they have received more intense training in their specific craft, and are savvy about the latest styles and processes.

If you have super-curly, very straight, or just generally unruly hair, ask the receptionist if there is someone who specializes in styling that particular texture. Better yet, find a stylist who has that particular texture, too. For example, Peg and I both have very curly hair and trust only other curly-haired peeps with our locks because we know they understand the problems, such as how it will shorten up 10 cm after it dries. Additionally, certain cuts and products work better than others for specific hair textures, and if the stylist has similar hair, she will know what works best.

Now that you know what to book and who to book it with, let's talk about *when* to book this day of hair therapy. Remember,

Diva, the process of getting your hair colored *always* takes much longer than the hairdresser says it will. In fact, it's not uncommon to spend two or more hours in the salon to get the shade just right. So plan ahead, and make sure you don't have to be somewhere else at a specific time after the salon. We also strongly advise you not to plan on flying anywhere the same day as a hair appointment: altitude = frizz for curly hair and static for straight hair, both deadly enemies for Divas! If you do have a specific time you must be out of the salon, tell the receptionist and your stylist before booking. They will usually do their best to let you leave on time.

Whether you're stuck there for hours or minutes, the salon is usually a fun escape from your daily grind. Think of it this way: where else can you discuss the latest celeb gossip and boyfriend drama and walk away with a fabulous 'do?

BUDGET CUTS

If you're on a tight budget, book a salon training session where a new stylist cuts your hair while a pro oversees. It can take longer, but you still get a great new cut without the big price tag. Another trick to getting a cost-effective coiffure is offering to promote your super-secret favorite stylist to all your Diva friends. Salons almost always have some sort of reward for referrals, nabbing you all kinds of discounts on services and products.

From Your Hair Down to Your Toes

Is there a chip in your manicure? Are your feet like Fred Flintstone's after using his "brakes"? Well, Diva, it must be nail time! You can do your mani/pedi combo at home, at a nail salon, or even at a spa. It all depends on your schedule and your budget.

Tight on money? Buy everything you need at a drugstore or beauty counter, and with a steady hand you can do it yourself. If you don't know what to get, splurge on a professional mani/pedi, and instead of dozing off pay close attention to what's used and what's done. With your newfound knowledge, the supplies you buy can last as long as three months, and that's a great way of saving money for your nonfat-triple-whip-must-have-daily-or-someone-will-die morning latte!

Never could color inside the lines as a child? Then forget DIY, and go to a local nail salon. This is an economical way for Divas who chip their manicures within a week to keep up their nails professionally, and essential for those who are simply no good at doing their digits themselves.

Ready for some spoiling? Spa manicures and pedicures are the *best* way to treat yourself. They're not that much more money and getting your feet rubbed is Earth's equivalent to a day in heaven. Nail treatments are already part of your general beauty regime, so treating yourself to something a little more decadent is a nice way to fit in some much-needed pampering. See how easily we justify it, Diva?

The Spa

This is a Social Diva's favorite place to be—although shoe shops run a close second. Most of the facilities are communal, so it's possible to meet new people, relax, and socialize all at the same time. Now *that's* multitasking, Diva!

Where to Book

Day spa: This is the traditional relax and pamper yourself place (think Bliss Spa or Spa Sydell). Day spas generally offer a menu of treatments ranging from borderline clinical to complete relaxation. Waxing, wraps, massages, facials, peels…you name it, and a day spa probably offers it. Treatments are generally performed by licensed beauticians and massage therapists, so that means you'll owe them a tip at the end of your service (but it's so totally worth it for all that relaxation).

Health spa: A visit to a health spa usually involves at least a couple of days in a beautiful location. The idea is to get away from all the stress in your life and indulge in cleansing therapies, relaxing treatments, and wonderful food in the midst of gorgeous countryside. They're a bit more clinical than day spas and often employ doctors as well as beauty therapists, so you'll get the best advice on how to keep yourself in great shape.

Med spa: These spas specialize in diagnosing the needs of your skin and treat your face accordingly. The therapists can also recommend an in-between regime to enhance your everyday look, which will extend the amount of time you need between visits.

Another bonus? Most med spas are run by doctors, so you are not required to tip; in fact, it is not even allowed. And that extra money you save can go toward those recommended products you'll want to buy to keep your skin Diva-beautiful.

Turkish baths and saunas: These are havens of relaxation and detoxification, and we highly recommend that you spend at least half a day in them. You will definitely be selling yourself short if you try to get in and out quickly, though judging from our experience, there's a good chance you'll never want to leave. (You've been warned!)

Turkish baths have steam rooms of various temperatures. You work your way up to the hottest, and then, if you can bear it, plunge into a cold pool between each one. The sauna works on a similar principle, but you can increase the temperature by throwing more water on the hot stones. The idea with both steam baths and saunas is that you stay in them long enough to sweat out your toxins. When you've had enough, you finish with a cold plunge—and yes, Divas, it is indeed *cold*—and then you head off to the massage room.

There, a therapist exfoliates your skin with an abrasive mitt, which feels better than it sounds, then massages you with soapy oil and rinses it away. Finally, you dry off in the frigidarium, a cool relaxation room with comfy loungers where you can snooze, chat, or read. You'll feel more relaxed than you ever thought possible!

H2O-LA-LA!

Heat treatments massage more toxins out of your muscles, but they are dehydrating, so drink plenty of water to feel your best both during and after.

What to Book

Exfoliating, extraction, cleaning, peels, and relaxations are all great reasons to see your esthetician for a facial on a monthly basis. There are many different kinds of facials, masks, and add-ons, so as to which service you should book, it depends on what your skin needs. We suggest discussing your skin issues with a dermatologist, beauty therapist, or esthetician before you book anything, but here is some general information about different facials and treatments that have worked wonders for us!

Chemical peel: This is an easy way of keeping your face clean and firm. We're not advocating the heavy-duty peels you see on television in *10 Years Younger*. We're talking about a light peel that lifts off only the outermost layer of dead skin. It can feel a bit tingly and uncomfortable, but the sensation lasts for less than two minutes, and the result makes it totally worthwhile.

Deep cleansing: This usually involves steaming, then extracting blackheads. Extractions are done during a basic facial. After your makeup has been cleaned off, a steamer will be placed near your face until the pores are open enough for the esthetician to go in for the kill. Sometimes this can be painful, but it's worth it,

Divas, we promise! Afterward, your skin will look fabulous—and you might even look a couple of years younger.

STAY-AT-HOME DIVA

Do not, we repeat, do not schedule an evening out after a facial. Your face feels so clean that the last thing you want to do is put makeup on it (although you can if you wish). Sometimes estheticians recommend not making any important plans for two days post-facial, just in case some imperfections come to the surface. If you're getting a peel, you might be flaky for a couple of days, so don't go scheduling any close-ups the day after a treatment, OK?

To Buy or Not to Buy?

Some places do a hard sell on the beauty products they use for facials, but bear three things in mind. First, don't feel you *have* to buy anything that your esthetician recommends. Second, know yourself. If it's suggested that you purchase an elaborate, five-step daily process and you know you'll never use it, tell the esthetician that the regime doesn't suit your style and see if she can recommend something else. Third, if your esthetician advises you to buy basic products, such as moisturizers or toners, take note of the active ingredients in them and compare them with what you already have at home. If you don't have anything similar, save yourself some cash by purchasing a product with the same active ingredient from your local drugstore.

Divas Don't Do Knots

Head, neck, shoulders, a little lower please…a massage is an excellent way to rejuvenate, detox, and relax your body, but be sure to book a massage that truly addresses your needs. Are your muscles super-tight with knots like rocks? Are you generally mellow but want to relax a bit more? Do you want to detox, exfoliate, and replenish your body's moisture? There are *sooo* many choices in terms of massage that it can be difficult to choose. Here's a breakdown of some of the most popular rejuvenating treatments.

Acupuncture: OK, so acupuncture isn't massage, but it's an absolutely fantastic way to un-knot your muscles and relax your mind. During this procedure, thin needles are inserted at particular points along the meridian lines of the body according to your personal needs. This can un-knot muscles, free you of headaches, and even get rid of acne…and afterward you'll feel like you're floating in a state of bliss.

Body scrub: You get two for the price of one with this treatment. Sea salts and sugars are gently rubbed all over your body to exfoliate the skin, and this has the added bonus of making any toxins take a hike! Scrubs are wonderfully invigorating and leave you feeling peachy clean.

Deep-tissue massage: The therapist works your muscles deep and hard in this treatment. Depending on how knotted you are, it can sometimes feel bruising or painful. Look past the pain because you will leave minus your knots, and that really is worth it, Diva.

Hot-stone massage: Ooh la la, this one is simply divine! Photos of this treatment can be misleading, as it appears that the therapist simply places lava stones on different energy chakras of your body and then instructs you to "say cheese!" In actuality, they first give you a serious rubdown with massage oil, and the stones feel amazing! They are heated, so when they rub across the oil that is already on your body, the oil becomes heated as well, and you feel as though you are being lathered from head to toe with amazing goodness from the pleasure gods.

Reflexology: This is type of massage specifically targets the pressure points on the feet, hands, or ears. Besides feeling divine, there is a belief that working on these key pressure points can have healing effects on other areas of the body as well. Bonus!

Swedish massage: This is a bit lighter than a deep-tissue massage. You still get the benefits of a nice rubdown, but the therapist is a tad gentler.

CASE THE JOINT

When booking a massage appointment, ask about any other facilities offered. Is there a steam room, sauna, showers, lockers, hairdryers? This way, you know exactly what you can take advantage of before or after your treatment. Give yourself plenty of time after your massage to take in the benefits of the spa. There is no reason to be in a rush when you are there to relax.

SPA DIVAS ARE SUPER-PUNCTUAL

Arrive early for your spa appointment (we suggest by at least fifteen minutes) because arriving right on time means you're already late. You have to change into a gown, then you have to fill out forms...before you know it you've lost fifteen minutes of rubdown time, and that, Diva, is a tragedy!

A Social Diva takes care of herself just as much as she has fun. Find the routine that works for you. Listen to your body, check your calendar, and make pampering at home, at a salon, or at a spa a regular part of your routine.

Now that you are rejuvenated, Diva, you can hit the party circuit again!

SOCIAL DIVA SPA ETIQUETTE

No cell phones, ever! There is nothing more annoying than hearing half a conversation when you are trying to relax. Don't be that person, ever!

Spa voices, please. Nothing is more fun than a spa day together with another Diva. And, of course, you are going to discuss your latest love or not-so-great date, but please whisper while you do it. Others are trying to relax, too, so be a good Diva and let them enjoy their downtime.

Don't stare at the naked people! Some, if not most, people are very uncomfortable being in their birthday suit in front of others, so keep your eyes on other people's eyes, Diva!

YOU LOOK FABULOUS (AND WE'RE NOT JUST SAYING THAT)

How a Social Diva Signs Off

Aww…look at you, Diva! All grown up and lookin' mighty fine, if we do say so ourselves!

Now that your wardrobe crises are part of the past, accessory calamities are gone with the wind, and dilemmas such as deciding on the choicest spot to cradle your cell phone during a Stones concert are out like a gem sweater with shoulder pads—you can officially consider yourself a true-blue, bona fide Social Diva! We're so proud of you, we're practically welling up! (But we are so not about to cry tears of joy over it because that would destroy our fabulous eye makeup.)

Check how much you've learned by referring back to the Test Your Diva-ness quiz on page 18 and see if you score higher than when you took it the first time: you know you will!

Oh, and don't give yourself lines worrying if you'll be able to remember all the tips and tricks we've discussed in these chapters. You can always refer back to this handy-dandy Diva guide, or stay tuned to ***www.socialdiva.com***, whenever you feel lost among the rows of designer shoes (or in any other fashion-overload moment you experience in the near future). In fact, we suggest you carry this book in your bag at all times…just in case!

Just don't forget that being a Social Diva starts from within. A positive attitude and self-confidence will get you far in life, and if you're going to live it on the outside, you've got to be it on the inside first!

And with that, we're ready to send you off into the action-packed social world—we know you're ready to go it all on your own!

Remember, Diva: you look fabulous—and we're not just saying that!

Acknowledgments

Peg's acknowledgments

Building Social Diva has been my passion, and it has also been a ton of hard work. I'd like to thank those who have supported me in this journey of following my dream to make it a success. Aunt Louise, thank you for listening to me as I go on, and on, and on again—and more important, for being interested in what I had to say. Uncle Merritt, thank you for being a rock and letting me know that I always have a place in your heart. Both of you are in mine. My darling Christine, my best, "no judgment," live-life-to-the-fullest friend and friend for life. Randomly as we met, it was meant to be. I am so blessed to have you in my life, and your energy and support has always been a light in my life. A special shout-out to my spiritual running buddies Brooke Emery, Karen Salmansohn, Gabrielle Bernstein, and Lizzie Love! I (almost) have no words; I honor the love and support you have provided me. I am truly grateful to have you in my life.

Thank you to many, many Social Diva supporters: you all have believed in me, especially during the times I wanted to give up. Thanks to the Divas Kimberly, Erin, Jackie, Karen, Renee, Becky, and Jill. Thanks to the whole crew at TAN, Ladies Who Launch, Divas Who Dine, and the Glasshouse Team. Thank you to my dot.com friends—Peter, Teresa, Michele M, MP, Scott, Amy A, Dave, and Skip. We share a crazy addiction to being online, but also know the value of an offline brand.

To my ATL crew—Jay, More Bill, Rebeca, Dusho, Allison, Dorothea, Neil, Lamar, KT, Tracy, Kirky, Johnny, Mason, Sari, Jobe, Vantosh, Oliver, Michelle, and Jason—who all know what

Nomenclature, Wednesday Night Bump Night, and "back in the day" really mean. And the rest of the people with whom I had hours and hours of fun "researching" for this book, you all know who you are and behind which velvet rope or inside which VIP room we've hung out.

To Lexi, baby Diva—you are a rock star! Your energy is amazing, you always make me laugh, and I am privileged to call you my friend and co-author. Hey, us Jersey girls have to stick together!

To all the places that let me camp out for hours of typing: Subtle Tea NYC, Soho House, and the Glenn Hotel in Atlanta (thank you for the upgrade)!

Now let's raise our glasses of champagne and have a toast to the launch of this book! Enjoy!

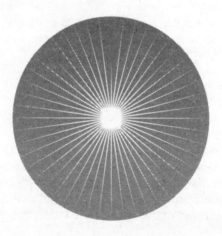

Lexi's acknowledgments

First and foremost, I have to thank my wonderfully supportive family for always believing in me and never hesitating to tell me so. Mom—thanks for blessing me with your trend-spotting gene, and for being my number one fan. You call me your star, but I couldn't shine if it weren't for you. Daddy—thanks for teaching me the importance of the metaphor, and for the note you wrote me while I was in college (it meant a lot more than you could ever know). I'll always be your Baby Bird. To The Joe—thanks for always participating in my ridiculous antics, and for being a friend when I was sad and you were passed out! Cobra Kai, Do-or-Die! To Adam—my Boofa—thank you for being my heart. Your pipe cleaners mean more than any diamond ever could. You are the sunshine of my life, that's why I'll always be around. To Colleen—my little Mutton Chop, you are an inspiration to all those around you, and that includes me, too. Thank you for your friendship, it's been and continues to be one of the most important things in my life, and one of the only things I know I can always count on. Your calves look spectacular, and I'll meet you in the bathroom. To Stephie—my little Rebel Rouser—thanks for always being a knock on the wall away, for being my wingman, and giving me *plenty* to write about. To E-Rock and Mari Mar—if it wasn't for our friendship, I wouldn't have been able to write this book. You don't even knoooow! To Kelly, Kelly, Kelly—thanks for always expecting utter awesomeness from me; it keeps me on my toes. I promise to bring you with me on tour, but only if I can borrow your Marc Jacobs boots. To all my pals at Ross Media—I'll meet you out back for a celebratory smoke. Oh, and Bill, don't forget that you have the power of the "glow," and I need to borrow it next weekend. To Peggy—thanks for always thinking of me first—you're the very definition of Social Diva.

I'd also like to give a shout-out to some who made this book possible: the crew at the Mansell Road Starbucks, Snyder's of Hanover, the Miller Brewing Company, O.P.I. Nailpolish, Ardel, and the fine people who make Parliament cigarettes.

Finally, to all the rest of my family and friends, thank you for all the pep talks, high-fives, and other miscellaneous renderings of support!

Catch the rest of you at Happy Hour!

Social Diva acknowledgments
We'd like to thank the crew at all the Diva-licious places we frequent (there are just too many to name here, but you all know who you are). Your fresh ideas are so brilliant, they make us proud to give you virtual ink. Keep up the good work!

Of course, we couldn't keep doing this without our advertisers, sponsors, and digital agencies. Keep spending money with us! Ha ha! We'll keep giving you the best audience for your products, services, or clients ever! (Yes, that means ever.)

To our dear lawyer and friend Michael: MTV, thanks for always watching out for a Social Diva's behind, and keeping your retainer (generally) low!

To our visionary web designers, for taking the idea of Social Diva and, through true talent, turning it into a visual brand:

Tribal Chicken Designs, you simply rock!

To those who help us look our best—Gucci, M.D.Skincare, Benefit, Kathlin Argiro, Ingwa Melero, Funky La La, Travel Jersey, and to all the PR mavens out there—keep sending us swag!

To all the Divas who inspire us to be our most fabulous, including (but not limited to): Donatella Versace, Diana Ross, Cher, David Bowie, Sophia Loren, Rita Hayworth, Jean Harlow, Bette Davis, Katherine Hepburn, Elton John, Tina Turner, Donna Summer, Patty LaBelle, Diane Von Furstenberg, Madonna, and Coco Chanel.

And last, but never the least, to all our friends and family: your undying love and support is what made all this possible for us—thank you from the very bottom of our stilettos!